THE MOST HATED MAN IN HOCKEY

Gary Bettman and Corporate NHL

J. Alexander Poulton

OVER TIME BOOKS

First printed in 2013 10 9 8 7 6 5 4 3 2 1
Printed in Canada

The Publisher: OverTime Books is an imprint of Éditions de la Montagne Verte

Library and Archives Canada Cataloguing in Publication

Poulton, J. Alexander (Jay Alexander), 1977–, author
The most hated man in hockey: Gary Bettman and Corporate NHL / J. Alexander Poulton.

ISBN 978-1-897277-79-9 (pbk.)

1. Bettman, Gary, 1952–. 2. National Hockey League—Biography. 3. Sports executives—United States—Biography. I. Title.

GV848.5 B49P69 2013   796.962092   C2013-903344-0

Project Director: Deanna Moeller
Editor: Kathy van Denderen
Cover Image: ©Lucas Jackson/Reuters/Corbis
Back Cover: Hockey Net: © Christian Amman / Photos.com
        Pile of Pucks: © grandeduc / Photos.com
        Gary Bettman: © Lucas Jackson / Reuters / Corbis

We acknowledge the financial support of the Government of Canada through the Canada Book Fund (CBF) for our publishing activities.

 Canadian   Patrimoine
Heritage   canadien

PC: 1

Contents

Dedication

To my wife and my baby

Two Different Scenes

June 1993 Stanley Cup Finals:
Montreal versus Los Angeles

It was the National Hockey League's 75th anniversary, and after a long season, the only two teams left standing were the Montreal Canadiens led by goaltender Patrick Roy and the Los Angeles Kings led by Wayne Gretzky. It was no surprise that the superstar-laden Los Angeles Kings had made it into the Stanley Cup finals, but the Montreal Canadiens were a team of young upstarts with only one superstar, Patrick Roy. The two teams were not exactly who the NHL marketing department would have liked to see in the playoffs, but the series still had the makings of excellent drama.

The Canadiens started their push into the playoffs finishing third in their division without a single player in the top 20 in scoring. In the first round of the playoffs, they faced their provincial nemesis the Quebec Nordiques, who had completely dominated them during the regular season. Things appeared to be going sour for the Habs from the outset, losing the first two games in Quebec City. The Canadiens, though, were able to rally from the series deficit with a pair of overtime wins to beat the Nordiques in six games. Those two wins started an incredible sudden-death winning streak that helped the Habs dispense with the Buffalo Sabres in the next round in four games straight, three of which ended in extra time. The Canadiens then defeated the New York Islanders in the Conference finals in five games, adding two more overtime wins for good measure.

The Canadiens watched with eager anticipation as the Los Angeles Kings and the Toronto Maple Leafs battled through an entertaining seven games. The 1992–93 season was one of the worst of Gretzky's career. He had spent most of the season out with a back injury and did not look like the Gretzky many people were used to seeing. But as the playoffs began, the old Gretzky began to emerge, and he helped lead the Kings through wins over the Calgary Flames and the Vancouver Canucks before coming up against a determined Toronto Maple Leafs.

In the first few games, it appeared as though Gretzky's back problems were resurfacing, keeping him from making any impact in the series. Facing elimination in game six against the Leafs, the Kings captain sprang to life at the right moment, as all great hockey players seem to do. After potting the game-six overtime winner, Gretzky played in one of the greatest games of his career, two days later. Before a rowdy Toronto crowd hoping their beloved Leafs would make it into the Stanley Cup finals for the first time since they last won the Cup in 1967, Gretzky quickly silenced the building when he finished a pretty give-and-go passing play with Marty McSorley on a short-handed break. Hopes of a Canadiens–Leafs final began to fade even faster when Gretzky made a beautiful pass to Tomas Sandstrom to make it 2–0 before the end of the first. The Leafs tied up the game in the second, but the captain put the Kings ahead once more with a classic Gretzky slap shot. In the third, with the Kings leading 4–3 with just three minutes remaining in the game, Gretzky finished off his night by scoring a hat trick. It was all the Kings needed to advance into the Stanley Cup finals to face Montreal.

Going into the first game of the final, odds-makers heavily favored the Los Angeles Kings. They were loaded with hockey stars Luc Robitaille, Wayne Gretzky, Rob Blake, Jari Kurri, Tomas Sandstrom and Tony Granato to name a few, while most hockey fans could barely name more than three on the Canadiens' roster. The Habs did have some good scoring up front led by Vincent Damphousse and Brian Bellows, but despite its deficiencies, the unit was solid and came together around the goaltending of Patrick Roy.

The first game on the hallowed ice of the old Montreal Forum went to the elite Kings squad, who completely dominated all aspects of the game, going on to win 4–1. The turning point of the series came in game two when the Kings were up 2–1 with just 1:45 remaining. Montreal Canadiens head coach Jacques Demers paced behind the bench, wondering what he could do for his team.

Earlier in the game, some of his players had noticed something fishy about the curve on Kings defenseman Marty McSorley's stick, and Demers wisely held onto the information. Now with under two minutes left to go, Demers called over referee Kerry Fraser and asked him to verify McSorley's stick for an illegal curve. Fraser took McSorley's stick and went to measure the blade in the penalty-box area. Demers waited impatiently while the referee deliberated with the other officials. Demers' hunch was right: the stick had an illegal curve, and McSorley was assessed a two-minute minor for the offense.

With nothing to lose, Demers pulled his goaltender out in favor of an extra attacker for a six-on-four power play. Montreal defenseman Eric Desjardins scored the equalizer from the point to force overtime. Desjardins then scored at 51 seconds into the overtime period to extend the Canadiens' overtime winning streak to eight straight games. It was the turning point of the series. The Canadiens followed that overtime win with two more before closing out the series in Montreal in game five with a 4–1 victory. It was Montreal's 24th Stanley Cup victory. It seemed rather fitting that on the 75th anniversary of the NHL, the league's new commissioner, Gary Bettman, would hand the Cup to the city that had basically owned the Cup through much of those 75 years.

As the Canadiens celebrated on the ice, the Conn Smythe Trophy and the Stanley Cup were escorted out to center ice by a young-looking Gary Bettman. After presenting the Conn Smythe Trophy to Patrick Roy, Bettman gave a short congratulatory speech to the city and the team, for which he received polite applause. He then handed the Stanley Cup over to the Habs' captain Guy Carbonneau. And thus Gary Bettman had wrapped up his first season as NHL boss. Sure, he had a few fires to put out that season, as well as a Stanley

Cup riot to deal with (where there were literal fires to put out), but hockey fans seemed to give him a pass. It was a kind of "I got my eye on you. Best don't mess with my game, son!" attitude toward the commish. Fast forward to the 2011 Stanley Cup finals.

June 2011 Stanley Cup Finals: Boston versus Vancouver

It was a battle between two different styles of hockey. The Vancouver Canucks were a highly skilled, fast-skating hockey team led by the wonder twins Daniel and Henrik Sedin, while the Boston Bruins (not short on scoring talent, either) were known more as a physical team, not afraid to go into the corners and battle hard for pucks. All of Canada was watching closely, too, since it was the first time since the 2005–06 playoffs that a Canadian team had made it into the Stanley Cup finals. If the Canucks won, it would also be the first time since the Montreal Canadiens last received the Stanley Cup from then rookie commissioner Gary Bettman that a Canadian team was crowned champion and the Cup came home.

The Canucks were the top team in the league with 117 points overall and all the pressure to make good in the post-season. They faced off in the first round against their playoff nemesis the Chicago Blackhawks. The two clubs had met in both the 2009 and 2010 playoffs with the

Blackhawks sending the Canucks to the golf course on both occasions. This time, the Canucks came out on top, but only by the skin of their teeth, eking out a win with a goal by Alexandre Burrows in a seventh-game overtime thriller.

The Bruins themselves were lucky to get out of the first round. After going down 2–0 to the Montreal Canadiens in their series, the Bruins managed to come back and win in game seven with a goal by Nathan Horton in overtime to advance into the next round.

The Canucks then handily made their way past the Nashville Predators and the San Jose Sharks to finally make it into the Stanley Cup finals for the first time since their devastating loss in 1994 to the New York Rangers. The Bruins for their part, after struggling against the Canadiens, walked over the Philadelphia Flyers in four straight games, then were in tough against the Tampa Bay Lightning, needing seven games to defeat them and move on to the finals against the Canucks. This was Boston's first appearance in the finals since the Edmonton Oilers beat them in 1990.

The atmosphere before the series was electric. The city of Vancouver had just come off a successful Winter Olympics in 2010 and was hoping to add the icing on the cake with a Stanley Cup parade. All of Canada was rallying behind the

Canucks in their efforts to bring the Stanley Cup back to Canadian soil where so many of the nation's hockey fans believe it belongs.

Just before the start of the series on June 1, 2011, Gary Bettman announced that former player Brendan Shanahan would replace the league's head of discipline, Colin Campbell. The change was announced so swiftly because Campbell's son Gregory played for the Bruins, and the league did not want bias to creep into any of the decisions. The decision should have been made the moment Gregory Campbell entered the league, as many believe his father's decision not to hand Zdeno Chara a suspension for his ugly hit on the Montreal Canadiens Max Pacioretty on March 8, 2011, stemmed from Colin Campbell's close ties to the Bruins organization. It was a smart move by Bettman as a way to avoid any further accusations of impropriety.

With the puck about to drop for the first game of the finals, it was unclear as to what kind of series fans could expect. Would the Canucks try to match the Bruins physically, or would they use their skill advantage to dictate the game? Would both Vezina Trophy candidate goaltenders stand up and take control of the series? Would the superpests Brad Marchand and Alex Burrows turn the series into a penalty-filled affair? Would both teams play it safe and use the much-hated trap system? As it turned out, the series included a little bit of everything.

The first game was a goaltender's duel, with Tim Thomas and Roberto Luongo matching each other save for save. It appeared that neither would falter and that the game would go deep into overtime periods. But the Canucks Raffi Torres broke the ice with just 19 seconds remaining in the game after taking a brilliant pass from Jannik Hansen for a one-timer into the yawning cage.

"It was just as exciting as an overtime goal," Luongo said of Torres' winner. "There was not a lot of room on the ice, as we saw. At one point I thought we might be playing all night here."

In the second game, the ice opened up and provided for a little more offense, but again, both goaltenders were stellar as the game went into overtime tied at two. Then it was Alexandre Burrows' moment to shine. Right off the opening faceoff, Burrows took a pass from Daniel Sedin and broke into the Bruins zone with just the big Zdeno Chara and Tim Thomas in his way. Burrows managed to speed his way around Chara and put Thomas out of position for a beautiful wraparound goal just 11 seconds into the period. Despite the close nature of both games, the Canucks seemed poised to finally get their hands on the Stanley Cup, but as any fan of the team from 1994 knew, you don't celebrate until the final buzzer sounds.

Unfortunately for the Canucks, the third game in Boston would completely turn the series around in the Bruins' favor and give them the momentum moving forward.

Although the first period ended without a goal, an incident on the ice provided the spark the Bruins lacked in the first two games. At the five-minute mark of the first period, the Canucks Aaron Rome clobbered the Bruins Nathan Horton with a devastating open-ice hit that knocked the Bruins forward out cold. Rome was assessed a major penalty and a game misconduct on the play, while Horton had to be carried off the ice on a stretcher and taken to hospital.

The image of their teammate laid out on the ice ignited the Bruins and unleashed the sleeping giant. Although they didn't score on the ensuing five-minute power play, the Bruins scored four straight goals in the second period and added another four in the third to completely embarrass the Canucks with an 8–1 win. They followed that win with another decisive 4–0 victory in game four to even the series.

At this point, both teams basically hated each other, as did the fans. In the media and on the ice, jabs were sent back and forth, and the animosity began to show on the ice as the penalty minutes went from just 10 minutes in game two to 145 minutes in game three. If familiarity breeds contempt, then the two teams loathed each other by the end of game four.

Games five and six were equally fierce, with both teams hitting dirty (the Bruins were better at this), but the series all came down to the last game. Game seven in Vancouver's Rogers Arena was set to be a doozy. Fans gathered in downtown Vancouver, in bars, in parks—anywhere they could see the game—hoping Canada would once again hold the Cup.

The atmosphere inside the arena was electric, but it quickly faded when the Bruins opened the scoring, and they never looked back. The Canucks could not even slip a single puck past Tim Thomas, losing the game 4–0 despite outshooting the Bruins 37–21.

As the Bruins celebrated on the ice, the fans' response was a mix of boos and polite applause. The level of noise quickly increased when Gary Bettman walked out onto the ice and grabbed the microphone. Thousands of heartbroken Canucks fans focused their disappointment and hatred on the commissioner. As he handed out the Conn Smythe Trophy to Bruins goaltender Tim Thomas, the chorus of boos and audible chants of "Bettman sucks! Bettman sucks!" subsided for a bit and was replaced with polite applause, but then as Bettman tried to congratulate the Bruins on their win, he was unceremoniously drowned out again. However, he remained unfazed by the hatred spewing from the fans, a steely characteristic he had been forced to adopt in order to have survived this long as the NHL commissioner.

He kept his cool even when irate fans tossed full cups of beer in his direction, barely missing their diminutive target. The disappointed Canadian fans paused for a moment when the Stanley Cup was ushered out onto the ice, but as soon as Bettman tried to speak, the fans booed so loud that the arena's state-of-the-art sound system could not match their power. Boston Bruins captain Zdeno Chara did not realize that it was his time to receive the Cup and had to be motioned over to Bettman's side for the official presentation.

After they exchanged a few inaudible words, the 5-foot-6 Bettman and the 6-foot-9 Chara (add another three inches when he is in skates) posed for a picture, then the Bruins celebration began. Bettman was quickly ushered out of the hostile arena. He tried to brush off the hateful reception as being the Canuck fans' disappointment at losing such a hard-fought series. But there was more behind those boos than just normal frustration. Hating Bettman had become the norm.

In 1993, when the hockey world knew nothing of Gary Bettman, fans had applauded the new commissioner. But by 2011, after two lockouts (with a third one looming) and nearly two decades of his rational, evasive manner when speaking about hockey (and everything else for that matter), hating Bettman became as natural to fans as putting on their favorite team jerseys.

Introduction

If Gary Bettman were to look back at his 20 years as the head of the National Hockey League, he would naturally boast of all his accomplishments, from those first tentative days in office in 1993 to his current position as seasoned veteran of all hockey affairs. What would lie before him is a vast list of triumphs for which he has been universally lauded. Such achievements include transforming the NHL into a modern entertainment enterprise that pulls in billions of dollars annually, when it once was a professional sports backwater; turning the populace in the southern United States on to a strange game played on ice; and attaining the contractual goals that he was originally hired to accomplish. Those are the accomplishments he will remember one day when looking back over his tenure as NHL commissioner, hoping to be thought of in the annals of sports history as a visionary.

However, many will look at that same period of the NHL under Bettman's rule and see his time as commissioner in a different light. From the moment he took office, Bettman has had his detractors. The common complaint about Bettman in the beginning was that he was an outsider to the game, and outsiders don't understand the nature of hockey.

He was a New York City lawyer that worked in a law firm until he was hired into the National Basketball Association. Growing up, he had seen a few NHL games and watched a handful of college games during his student days, but that was the extent of his hockey IQ. When he was first hired, Bettman kept a copy of Ken Dryden's book *The Game* so he could better understand what hockey meant to fans that loved the sport and didn't view it simply as a commodity to be sold.

This separateness from the culture of hockey is something that has dogged him throughout his tenure as NHL commissioner. The questions were always the same. How could someone make decisions about the very nature of the game if they didn't understand it on a deeper level and go through the battles that the players undertake in their path toward the NHL? This outsider image of Bettman is something that has only grown as the seasons pass, and even after 20 years as NHL boss, he is still tagged as someone who doesn't understand the game.

During the lockouts, players were often quick to point out that Bettman did not understand what the game was about and what the players had to contend with. However, to be fair to Bettman, those things really didn't matter. Although he tried to understand the game on a deeper level and attended hundreds of games over the course of his career, his ultimate allegiance was to the people who hired him—the team owners.

Maybe it was Bettman's lack of understanding of the nature of the game that led him to try to market the sport like a Hollywood blockbuster movie when he first joined the league in 1993. He ran a series of bad commercials that had little to do with hockey—they seemed more like commercials for cologne rather than a sport, and he allowed the Fox Network to get away with the "FoxTrax Puck," which replaced the black puck on Americans television screens with a glowing, colored comet.

In his defense, however, Bettman was marketing the game to a whole new audience in the United States, one that knew little about the game. He had to try new ways of pushing the sport onto city populations that suddenly found they had a hockey team. In places like San Jose, Dallas and

Phoenix—cities more likely to be the backdrop of a Clint Eastwood western rather than a winter sport—Bettman had to attract a regular audience to the game of hockey. He was bound to have a few failures along the way.

The biggest issue for his critics wasn't the minor changes he made, but the fact that he was pushing the game into markets that had no prior hockey culture. North Carolina and Phoenix were devoid of a population with any hockey knowledge (save for a few Canadian retirees), while in Canada, whose population knew everything about hockey and had turned it into a religion, franchises were struggling and even closing their doors. To many critics of Bettman, he was only going after the money and forgetting about the heart of the game.

Gary Bettman wasn't perfect. He never claimed he was. His mandate was to take hockey to new heights, something that had never been tried before his arrival. Before Bettman, the NHL operated like a sleepy family business, and just a few years into his job, he had turned the fortunes of the league into a large corporation. Trying to inject new ideas into a league that historically rejected any major changes was bound to bring out the critics. As hard as it was to see teams like the Quebec Nordiques and the Winnipeg Jets fly south, the NHL has grown incredibly under Bettman and has pulled in record profits.

These examples, however, are like tiny drops in a bucket when trying to explain why so many people don't like Gary Bettman. The true hatred for the man really surfaced during the first lockout in 1995 and achieved new heights when the season was cancelled in 2004–05. Although Bettman had always claimed he was operating in the best interest of the game, it was hard to see the logic behind losing hockey games, and Bettman became the whipping boy for all those frustrations. Many rational people could see during the contract negotiations with the National Hockey League Players Association that certain issues needed to be fixed to see the sport flourish. But after three lockouts in 20 years, the little sympathy Bettman had in the beginning has long since been destroyed.

No matter what side of the fence you are on when it comes to Gary Bettman, remember this: his contract will one day end, and he will walk out of the office of the NHL commissioner. The only thing left for us to figure out when that day comes is how will history look upon him? Will he be considered the most hated man in hockey or the most necessary?

Chapter One

Before Bettman

The entire hockey world might not have many warm and fuzzy feelings for Gary Bettman, but before his arrival in 1993, the NHL was not a picture of rosy contentment. The league had its problems, a lot of them financial. A September 1993 article published in *Sports Illustrated* listed the worth of every franchise in the National Football League, National Basketball Association, Major League Baseball and the National Hockey League. It came as no surprise that at the top of the list were the New York Yankees, valued at $225 million, followed by three other baseball clubs at $200 million each. The NFL's most valuable franchise, the Dallas Cowboys, were in sixth place at $175 million, while Michael Jordan's champion Chicago Bulls topped the NBA in 20th spot overall with a value of $140 million.

If you ran an index finger down the list, you'd have to pass by 59 other franchises before hitting an NHL club. The Detroit Red Wings popped in at 60th place overall, valued at $80 million. The Ottawa Senators, Tampa Bay Lightning and the Winnipeg Jets were near the bottom of the list, valued at $35 million.

The National Hockey League was clearly a step behind the other major sporting leagues in North America. To make matters worse for the league, professional hockey was even further behind the other sports in annual ticket revenue and thousands of miles behind in broadcasting dollars to the point where the NFL was making billions while the NHL picked up the scraps of a few hundred million. I'd mention the NHL's merchandise revenue, but that figure is embarrassing compared to the over $2 billion brought in by the NBA.

The problem in the NHL in the early '90s was that it was stagnating, suffering from the "old boys club" culture that had been ingrained into hockey since well before the league's formation in 1917. Prior to the existence of the National Hockey League, the Montreal Canadiens, Montreal Wanderers, Ottawa Senators, Quebec Bulldogs and Toronto Blueshirts existed under the umbrella of the National Hockey Association (NHA). The NHA had a series of disputes with the owner of the Blueshirts, Eddie Livingstone, so the other league owners decided to disband the league and form their own, rather than dealing with the problem franchise.

In 1917, a new Toronto club called the Arenas joined the Montreal Canadiens, Montreal Wanderers and Ottawa Senators to form the National Hockey League. Once the pesky Livingstone was out of the way, the league could operate as the established owners saw fit. This owners-first culture flourished and entrenched itself into the NHL boardrooms, and the office of the president of the NHL operated something like the papacy. The league's first president, Frank Calder, held onto the position until his death in 1943. Red Dutton was named acting president and eventually assumed the role of the presidency in 1945 only to hand over the job in 1946 to his assistant Clarence Campbell, the next infallible pope of the league (1946–77).

From 1946 to the early 1960s, the NHL enjoyed its most stable period, known as the "Original Six" era. The old-guard franchises flourished, the players were elevated to the status of gods (in the case of Maurice Richard and Gordie Howe), and the league had complete control over all of the business, paying the players a meager workman's salary. If Frank Calder had been seen as a tough, unmoving stone on issues, Clarence Campbell was 10 times worse.

Campbell dealt out the harshest suspension to any player in his 31 years on the job as NHL boss when he had the nerve to suspend Montreal Canadiens superstar Maurice Richard for the remainder of the season and the playoffs in 1955. He upped the ante when he showed up at the next Canadiens home game following the announcement of the suspension. To say Canadiens fans were a little upset by the brazen disrespect for their prized player would be an understatement. Throughout the game, Campbell sat in his Montreal Forum seat and did not flinch at the barrage of insults, paper balls, magazines and beverage cups thrown his way. He even stood up to one thug who directed a punch at him. It took a smoke bomb thrown by an irate fan to move Campbell from his seat.

But this stalwart of the league status quo who would have kept the NHL on its path for years to come finally opened up and decided to expand the NHL from the original six to twelve teams. It might have seemed to be a big leap for Campbell to take, but he did not make the decision of his own free will.

In the late 1950s, the Western Hockey League (WHL), which included the Calgary Stampeders, the Edmonton Flyers and the Brandon Regals, decided to expand further into the United States.

The WHL opened up franchises in Los Angeles, San Diego and San Francisco with future plans to establish itself as a major league and compete for the Stanley Cup. With arenas capable of holding 10,000 fans, and with plans underway to build bigger and better arenas, there was enough talent to match the competitive teams in the NHL. After watching to see if the WHL could maintain the teams' viability, Campbell was forced into action. In 1965, he announced that the league would be adding six new teams in 1967–68, including teams in Los Angeles and Oakland. The news hampered the WHL's progress and eventually led to it folding in 1974.

The NHL continued its expansion through the 1970s partly as the result of the rise of another rival league, the World Hockey Association (WHA). By the end of the 1979–80 season, the NHL had 21 teams. Despite the influx of new team owners into the NHL, behind the scenes, the league remained the sleepy backwater of professional sports.

Campbell, who was still at the helm in the mid-1970s, kept the league mired in the Original Six era of thinking and doing business. As time went on, it became apparent that he was less interested in the day-to-day operations of the company and was putting more emphasis on his side business projects, including a deal for all the concessions at Montreal's Dorval Airport. He also closed the NHL head office for the entire month of July, effectively shutting down all league business.

Campbell was eventually pushed out of his job as NHL president in 1977, but the incumbent John Ziegler did little to foster a new corporate atmosphere. When the former WHA teams were incorporated into the NHL during the 1979–80 meetings, the team executives were shocked to discover that the annual board of governors meeting was held in an ultra-luxurious Florida hotel where leisure activities included a croquet tournament and a fancy ball where the owners and their wives danced under a crystal chandelier to a 15-piece orchestra playing the tunes of Glenn Miller.

American John Ziegler saw the need for change the moment he stepped into the NHL's head office, but he found the going slow and tedious. The office was disorganized, and soon after finding the league accounting books, he discovered to his horror that the league was close to insolvency. The NHL was in jeopardy. The teams were not pulling in enough revenues, and its players' salaries were sky-rocketing because of pressures from the World Hockey Association, which was paying its players astronomical salaries averaging around $50,000 to $70,000 per year, whereas the average NHL salary was in the $30,000 range. The result was an exodus of players to the WHA who were not getting the money they felt they deserved from the NHL. The first volley in the salary war was sent in 1972 when the WHA's Winnipeg Jets signed Bobby Hull to a 10-year, $1 million salary. As a result of the inflation in players' salaries, the NHL was operating at a loss in the $100-million range.

The prickly team owners were Ziegler's main obstacle. The owners, for the most part, were happy with the status quo in the league and were not about to consent to change, especially any advice coming from some American lawyer who had only played some hockey in college.

This snobbish attitude toward Americans in hockey is something that permeated all levels of the game. Somehow, by virtue of being born north of the 49th parallel, it was assumed that Canadians had an innate knowledge and spirit for the game of hockey. This idea is still something that persists in the minds of most Canadians. Just ask any random guy watching a hockey game in a bar anywhere from Dildo, Newfoundland, to Victoria, BC, which country is better at hockey, and you'll most likely hear a litany of old myths and romanticisms about Canada's connection to the roots of the game.

John Ziegler had hoped that by ascending to the top of the league as president, he would be exempt from this Canadian bias. His most vocal critic during his tenure as NHL boss was the fiery Toronto Maple Leafs owner Harold Ballard, who openly called him names in the press and never held back his contempt for the "know-nothing." Even the press did not often give Ziegler a chance, calling him the "American-born president of the NHL."

Fortunately, for the health and well-being of the National Hockey League and its owners, Ziegler had tough skin. The best way to change a stubborn system, he quickly figured out, was to show results. He managed to turn NHL revenues from being well into the red to a healthy stream of profits, and more importantly, he lined the pockets of the established owners with expansion fees from the Edmonton, Hartford, Quebec, Winnipeg and later Ottawa and Tampa Bay franchises. In 1992, the same year Ottawa and Tampa Bay signed on the dotted line to pay the $50-million franchise fee, a group that wanted to set up a franchise in Hamilton, Ontario, led by Tim Hortons' boss Ron Joyce, dropped out of the franchise race because of the high entry price, crushing the province's need for a team other than the Leafs.

Despite producing some positive results, Ziegler was still *persona non grata* in hockey circles because of his hands-off approach to league management. He thought it best to be heard and not seen when it came to the day-to-day operations of the league, but owners and most of the press did not appreciate his absence. Ziegler rarely went to watch games during the regular season, and in terms of handing out discipline, he was less than effective. The most glaring example of this came during the 1988 playoff series between the New Jersey Devils and the Boston Bruins.

After getting hammered 6–1 by the Bruins in game three, New Jersey Devils head coach Jim Schoenfeld was noticeably frustrated and focused his anger on referee Don Koharski after the game. When the two came face to face in the hallway leading to the dressing rooms, Schoenfeld got in Koharski's face and appeared to slightly touch the referee, who stumbled on his skates into the wall. Koharski could be heard screaming, "You push me! You're done! And I hope it's on tape." To which Schoenfeld replied, "You're crazy. Ya, well good, 'cause you fell, you fat pig! Have another donut! Have another donut!"

The NHL Officials Association was fuming over the incident when Ziegler and the league failed to act, even in the slightest of ways. So in order to get the NHL's attention, the association refused to work the fourth game of the series just two days later. The threat was not taken seriously at first, and the league went ahead for the start of the game.

Players from both teams were on the ice warming before the game when players and coaches got word that the referees would not be coming out on the ice to drop the puck for the opening faceoff. In an incredible scene, both teams simply skated off the ice, leaving fans at the arena and at home wondering what was going on behind the scenes. Replacement referees were quickly ushered out onto the ice, wearing the usual striped shirts and orange armbands, but the linesmen came out wearing yellow jerseys.

The game eventually got underway with the scab referees, and the NHL officials frantically tried to remedy the embarrassing situation while the game was in progress. But it wasn't Ziegler who was involved in the sudden crisis—he left that task for his deputies to handle. A calamity was averted when the league capitulated to the demands of the irate referees and suspended Jim Schoenfeld for game five (which the Devils lost 7–1 and eventually the series in seven games).

After this incident, the owners' patience with Ziegler's ineffectiveness was growing thin. The business of hockey had taken a few steps forward, but it was far behind other sports leagues in North

America. The NHL still had the stigma of a professional sports backwater in comparison to the business and marketing machine being developed in the NFL, for example. It wasn't just the upper management that was failing; the game itself needed a major overhaul. Aging buildings were crumbling, dressing rooms looked liked Little League locker rooms compared to the luxury accommodations that today's players are used to, and the franchises operated with skeletal staff—in the smaller markets, you could find the director of marketing selling tickets in a booth come game time.

Players back then did not have anywhere near the luxuries they have today. Before the 1990s, NHL teams had to fly on commercial flights, which meant that they had to line up with all the other passengers (crying babies included) headed to their destinations and make connecting flights if necessary. Imagine Sidney Crosby sitting in a cramped coach seat eating pretzels and having to wake up the fat businessman next to him so he can go pee. Such traveling conditions drained players' physical health and affected their mental attitude if they had to play a game the next day.

Hockey was in need of a change, and the NHL owners would get the excuse they needed to make a change right before the 1992 playoffs.

From 1967 until 1991, the National Hockey League Players Association (NHLPA) enjoyed relative peace with the owners because its executive director, Alan Eagleson, had a comfortable relationship with many of the league owners. For years, those in the inner circles of the NHL knew that Eagleson was acquiring too much power as a broker between players, agents, owners and the media, and that he was using that power for his personal profit. But no one dared look into his dealings until 1990, when Russ Conway of the New England newspaper *The Eagle-Tribune* wrote several scathing exposés on Eagleson and revealed a high level of corruption, from the mishandling of players' pension funds to backhanded dealings with his owner friends. When all of these allegations came to light, the NHLPA got rid of Eagleson and installed former player-agent and deputy NHLPA director Bob Goodenow as executive director on January 1, 1992.

Goodenow's first task was to negotiate a new collective bargaining agreement with the NHL owners. The previous agreement had expired prior to the start of the 1991–92 season, on September 15, 1991. The meetings between Goodenow and NHL president John Ziegler began in late February and continued well into March, with no resolution in sight. There was a whole range of issues at stake in the negotiations, but the main sticking points for both sides were how free agency worked, the arbitration process, playoff bonuses, pensions and revenue from using the players' images on trading cards and in video games.

The players had a genuine gripe against the NHL owners in the contract negotiations. For example, in terms of bonuses, the team that lost in the first round of the playoffs paid each player $3000, and if the player was on the Stanley Cup–winning team, he was paid up to $25,000. This sum contrasted significantly with the owners' take of close to $500,000 per playoff game played.

The contract talks went on through March but with no progress. In order to put pressure on the owners to make some concessions, Goodenow and the NHLPA unanimously agreed to go on strike on April 1, 1992. They felt that with the owners' cash cow—the playoffs—under threat, the owners would have to quickly return to the negotiating table and begin to see things the players' way.

As the days in April began to fall away, Ziegler and the owners tabled what they deemed their "final offer" on April 7, but the NHLPA immediately rejected the deal. The next day, in a move that would become familiar to hockey fans, a federal mediator joined the discussions hoping to bring the two sides together. Although the two sides had agreed on most issues, the major roadblock for the owners was the players' demand of a share of the $16 million in trading card revenue annually. After long hours of talks, the NHL and the players finally agreed to a two-year contract that was retroactive to the beginning of the season, allowing for the remaining games to be played and for the playoffs to go ahead. As part of the deal, the season was expanded from 82 to 84 games, playoff bonuses for the players were dramatically increased and there were major changes to how free agency and arbitration worked.

Bob Goodenow called the strike a "major moment," stating, "I don't think the owners took the players seriously and it wasn't until the strike that they understood the players were serious."

For the time being, there was peace in the NHL, but with a short two-year agreement, the prospect of another strike or lockout seemed inevitable, as the owners were unhappy with the deal. They felt they had been forced into signing the agreement because of the looming possibility of cancelling the playoffs. As a result of the bum deal, the owners got together and removed John Ziegler as president of the league and replaced him with interim president Gil Stein until someone more suitable and amenable to the owners' needs could be found. But don't feel bad for Ziegler. He received a hefty $2-million payout and a $250,000 per year pension, and he didn't even leave the game. Chicago Blackhawks owner Bill Wirtz appointed Ziegler as the team's alternate governor, a role he still plays.

Gil Stein was not new to hockey. While working for a Philadelphia law firm, he was recruited by the Flyers in 1976 to become their chief operating officer and executive vice president. So when the NHL came calling in 1992, he was well prepared to take over the league's operations. Entering the position in June 1992, Stein immediately went about making changes to how the office of the NHL president did its business. One of Stein's first official duties was to take over the responsibility of handing out player punishment, a task that was previously handled by a vice president. When the 1992–93 season got underway, Stein also made himself visible to the public and the media, appearing at numerous games and making his office open to journalists. He didn't just sit in the office chair of the president to keep it warm for the next guy.

While Stein held the reins of the league, he involved himself in its future. He restructured the office and fired executives who had gotten too comfortable in their positions, and he even advocated among the owners that they allow their players to play in the 1994 Winter Olympics. The NHL president was also actively searching for his replacement, hiring an executive search firm to scour the corporate world for someone suitable.

Gil Stein did not have to look for long. Just over seven months later, the search ended when the league hired former senior vice president of the NBA, Gary Bruce Bettman.

Chapter Two

From NBA to NHL

Gary Bettman was born in Queens, New York, on June 2, 1952, a few months after the Detroit Red Wings defeated the Montreal Canadiens in four straight games to win the Stanley Cup. It was the era of the greats: Maurice Richard was at his peak, igniting the ice and the city of Montreal; Gordie Howe was young, scoring a lot and finishing off his own fights. It was an amazing time to be a hockey fan. Gary Bettman, though, wasn't watching. He had other interests, and like a good Jewish boy making his mother happy, he forged a path in his life that led him directly into law school, studying industrial and labor relations at Cornell University. That had always been the plan for Bettman growing up. He could have joined the family business, the Bettman Nut Company, but he preferred to go out into the world on his own. His parents divorced when he was just four years old, but his father remained a presence in his life until he died when Bettman was 13.

Gary Bettman was never much for playing sports during his childhood, though he did pick up a love of sailing from his father. He dabbled a bit in soccer, but he found more pleasure in debate clubs. Even at a young age, he was working toward obtaining a law degree.

Life at university was easy for Bettman. While the world around him was involved in the Vietnam War, cultural change, disco and drugs, Bettman had a decidedly country club experience in university. Instead of reading poetry or smoking drugs like his fellow students, Bettman was busy studying, involving himself in his fraternity and hanging out with friends. It was in university where he met his future wife, Shelli, mother of his three children, Lauren, Jordan and Brittany.

After graduating from Cornell, Bettman went on to get his Juris Doctor degree from the New York University School of Law in 1977. Fresh out of school and still wet behind those big ears, Bettman put on his best polyester suit and landed a job with Proskauer Rose Goetz and Mendelsohn, a law firm that specialized in labor and litigation law. It was while working for this law firm that he began his path toward becoming NHL commissioner.

Also working in the same office was one David Stern, future commissioner of the NBA and

Bettman's boss. There were also several other lawyers who played integral roles in the legal affairs
of the NHL, the NBA and the NFL. At the time,
though, 25-year-old Bettman was just a tiny fish
in an ocean of bigwig lawyers, and while other
lawyers moved up and onward to greater things,
Bettman remained a small-time lawyer in the
firm, pushing papers. Stern, a man that Bettman
looked up to, and for whom he pushed a few of
those papers, ended up leaving the firm, taking
a job as the general counsel to NBA commissioner
Larry O'Brien in 1978.

Two years later, Stern was named the executive
vice president of the NBA. Bettman could not see
it then, but Stern's ascension in the NBA would
end up benefitting him. From 1978 to 1980, Bettman languished as just another lawyer in New
York City and was desperately in need of a new
direction in his career. After putting in a few calls
to friends, someone mentioned that a job was
opening up in the legal department of the NBA. It
wasn't an executive position, but it would get Bettman out of the basement and into something
exciting. He began his career with the NBA in late
1980 as the assistant general counsel in all the
association's legal matters.

At the time of Bettman's arrival in the NBA,
the league was much like the NHL. Believe it or

not, Bettman was just one of the 25 people employed in the league's head office. Despite having superstars like Kareem Abdul Jabbar, Larry Bird and Magic Johnson, the NBA had a tough time getting fans into the buildings, and it was even harder for fans to watch the games on television because the networks did not want to air the sport on television. And when the NBA did make it on TV, it was all negative. Player brawls, stints in drug rehab or infidelities (I would argue that this part has not changed—cough, cough, Kobe) all led to the image of the NBA as a fringe league, more a curiosity than a real sport. These external problems contributed to the NBA's serious financial troubles by the time Bettman joined in 1980.

If there is one thing lawyers are good at, it is looking at the facts, and David Stern saw the writing on the wall and finally made some changes to save the NBA from going into bankruptcy. In the early 1980s, Stern approached the basketball players' union and presented them with the stark reality of the league if things continued with the status quo. It took a few months of intense negotiations, but Stern managed to convince the players to accept the first salary cap in pro sports history.

Bettman was watching eagerly from the sidelines. In return for accepting the cap, the players were guaranteed 53 percent of gross revenues (from TV, tickets sales and so on). With the new deal and the arrival of a certain "Air Jordan" in 1984, as well as Charles Barkley and John Stockton, the league completely turned around its fortunes. When Stern took over complete command of the NBA in 1984, he moved Bettman up the ladder to the third highest position in the league's legal department. This promotion brought Bettman into the inner workings of the deals; he participated and actively negotiated in collective bargaining agreements, licensing and the development of the NBA as a business all its own.

The arrival of a singular superstar like Michael Jordan really helped Stern and Bettman execute their jobs effectively. After a decade of negative attention in the media toward the NBA, people were now talking about Michael Jordan's airtime and his latest contract for running shoes. The new NBA became more palatable to the public and therefore more profitable. Bettman used that star power (as he would later use a young hockey player from Nova Scotia) to help make a new television deal with NBC. Bettman was also present to help oversee the expansion of the league into Charlotte, Miami, Minnesota and Orlando.

With the NBA finally on the right track, another league began looking to it for inspiration and help in its efforts to restructure and renew its business.

After ridding itself of John Ziegler in 1992, the team owners in the NHL got together and began their search for his replacement. The person leading the charge for new management was Los Angeles Kings owner Bruce McNall.

McNall was a new archetype of NHL owner. He was flamboyant, outgoing and willing to make a lot of noise to get business done. Prior to his arrival with the Los Angeles Kings, the team was not really the biggest draw in the region. Since joining the league in 1967, the team had a few seasons where they showed some potential, but they consistently failed to get the attention of the populace. When McNall wrestled the controlling stake of the team from the hands of former owner Jerry Buss, he knew the team needed something to attract the fans. His answer was to pull off the biggest trade in the history of the NHL to date.

After many months of secret talks, it was announced in the summer of 1988 that Edmonton Oilers forward Wayne Gretzky, Canadian icon, would be traded to the Kings along with Mike Krushelnyski and Marty McSorley in return for Jimmy Carson, Martin Gelinas, three first-round draft picks and about $15 million. The timing of this trade couldn't have come at a worse time for the Oilers. Gretzky's Oilers had just won the

Stanley Cup a few months earlier, and he had been voted the playoffs MVP.

While Canadians collectively scratched their heads over the deal, McNall had transformed the Los Angeles Kings overnight into the city's premiere attraction. Revenues increased, fans bought Kings jerseys like never before, and most importantly, celebrities turned out to watch the Great One perform his magic. The other team owners saw McNall's turnaround of the club as a sign that he should take the lead in the hunt for the new NHL boss.

Among the possible candidates for the position were the presidents and CEOs of large corporations—even Brian Mulroney was considered as he was officially out of work in September 1993. All the candidates were qualified on paper, but none of them had any sort of background in pro sports. McNall was of the opinion that the league needed a new outlook on the business of the game, and so he turned his sights to the redesigned NBA and its commissioner David Stern.

McNall presented Stern with a huge salary offer and a bonus package he thought would be hard to resist, but Stern flatly turned it down. McNall then inquired about the NBA's second-in-command, Russ Granik, but Stern refused to let him go.

Then Stern proposed that McNall talk to the third man in charge, Gary Bettman.

After meeting with Bettman, McNall knew that he had met the right candidate. As for Bettman, he knew the opportunity to go any higher in the NBA pretty much stopped at his job as things were moving along nicely under the leadership of Stern. So Bettman figured he would take a shot at the NHL.

Sure, Bettman did not have the stature of a hockey player; he was the complete opposite. He was a short Jewish American and had never played hockey on any level, not even Peewee. But McNall had confidence in Bettman. Now all Bettman had to do was convince the rest of the NHL team owners that he was the man for the job.

At a formal interview in front of several NHL owners, Bettman was grilled on labor talks, the salary-cap system, league expansion and taking the league into new business markets. Bettman wowed the owners with well-crafted, prepared answers. Suddenly, the little Jewish lawyer from New York was the front-runner. After the interview, the NHL dropped Gil Stein (he got a $500,000 per year consulting contract for five years to cushion his fall, on top of his annual $250,000 pension). On December 11, 1992, at the

NHL annual board of governors meeting in Palm Beach, Florida, it was made official that the 40-year-old New York City lawyer would become the next commissioner of the National Hockey League.

The news was not announced with much fanfare, however. It was typical of the NHL, actually. In a run-of-the-mill hotel banquet room, a few rows of chairs were set up for the media, and at the front table sat Bettman, McNall and Stein. Behind the trio, someone had affixed an old black-and-orange NHL pennant to a black curtain. After a few short statements from Stein and McNall, Bettman addressed the hockey world for the first time and laid out his agenda for the future of the league. "I believe that a commissioner has a responsibility to run the game as well as he can for the benefit of everyone; the owners, the players and the fans." Then he paused for a moment, let out a sly grin and continued, "The owners are my employer, but the way a league performs well is by making its product as attractive as it can to the greatest number of fans, and I believe that by making this sport as attractive as possible, as a sport and as an entertainment product that we will be in a position to satisfy all the needs, those of the owners, those of the fans and those of the players as well."

His statement and answers to the media were considerably lawyer-like, and as hockey reporters would come to know, very "Bettman-esque." When the question-and-answer portion of the telecast was complete, the new commissioner put on a three-sizes-too-big black-and-orange NHL All-Star jersey and flashed a big smile for the cameras. The photo looked a little odd; it was as if McNall and Stein were posing for a photo with a fan, as Bettman, positioned in the middle, was a lot shorter than the tall Stein and the wide McNall. Bettman might have just delivered a serious press conference, but his smile in that photo made him look like a kid in a candy store.

The fancy new title of "NHL Commissioner" came with an increase in power over that of the former presidents of the league. Former presidents like John Ziegler didn't have the authority Bettman now had. For example, when Toronto Maple Leafs owner Harold Ballard called Ziegler names and deliberately disobeyed his orders, Ziegler could do nothing in return. Bettman, on the other hand, could punish team executives and owners who fell out of line with league policy. Bettman also had the final word in resolving disputes among the franchises and in setting the future agendas of the league. Although some people heralded the arrival of Bettman, many more approached his appointment as league boss with extreme caution, especially the players.

When Bettman officially took over NHL operations on February 1, 1993, he faced a league needing a revolution in ideas but with a culture hesitant to accept it. The push-back against the new commissioner was immediate, led by an aggressive news media.

From the beginning, Bettman was pegged as the outsider, brought in to alter every aspect of hockey, from the way it was played to the way it was sold, for better or worse. Bob McKenzie of the *Toronto Star* wrote a full feature on the new commissioner with the headline blaring Bettman's quote, "Everything is under review." The statement was interpreted by the media as, "I am going to change it all!"

The one item from the interview with Bettman that got stuck in the media's head like an annoying pop song were the words "orange puck." It didn't matter that before he said "orange puck," he said, "I'm not looking at doing anything stupid, like using an..." It was a first lesson in dealing with the media, and he would not let his words slip so easily in the future.

When the media is skeptical about someone, they will pull out whatever piece of information in their minds that suits the narrative of that person and make it the truth. In his former job in the NBA, Bettman was insulated against personal attacks by the media. For all they knew, he was simply just another suit behind the scenes doing the bidding of the NBA commissioner. Now Bettman was up front and exposed, and he would have to get used to the scrutiny. Hockey was and still is an old boys club, and this American outsider would have to jump over the moon to prove himself.

In the 20 years since Bettman first took over as NHL commissioner, he has taken the game to new heights, and through it all, he has retained his steely resolve. He learned early on that in order to get the job done and ensure the survival of the league, he was going to have to step on a few toes. Plus, it's not like he was asking the hockey world to like him, though it is certain that he wouldn't mind a little appreciation every now and again. But he knew his position at the top would be lonely and would remain that way—no one ever really likes their boss, so he is content with the facts.

Since Bettman's arrival in the NHL, the game has reached greater heights in the sports entertainment world than ever thought possible. Team earnings have jumped from the millions into the billions. For example, the Toronto Maple Leafs recently were the first NHL club to be valued at over $1 billion. (Not bad for a club that didn't make the playoffs for seven years in a row.) Although there is a great disparity between what the Toronto Maple Leafs are worth and what the Phoenix Coyotes are valued at, Bettman has made a good portion of the league's owners richer, as he was hired to do.

Like it or not, Bettman has transformed the way the game is played, never getting stuck in the old way of doing things. The league head office that once closed for a month in the summer is now open for business 24/7. It previously operated like a corner mom-and-pop shop rather than a corporation, but it is now a globally recognized brand, pulling in millions of advertising dollars, and has a bright future.

Bettman was hired to bring some semblance of order to the league owners, and now the owners operate under his rules. Although he is not without his flaws and is still as loud and as obnoxious as some like to remind him, Bettman continues to do his job, drowning out the noise and preferring to focus on the task ahead. In his first few months in office, he would have a lot of noise to deal with that wasn't always easy to ignore.

Chapter Three

A New Direction

Gary Bettman's first season as NHL commissioner in 1993 was filled with ups and downs. A year after celebrating the 75th anniversary of the National Hockey League, it was now time for Lord Stanley's mug to celebrate its 100th year in existence. Just a few days into Bettman's new job, Montreal was hosting the NHL All-Star game at the Montreal Forum, and to help celebrate, the league called upon Canadiens legends Guy Lafleur, Maurice "Rocket" Richard and Jean Beliveau to carry in the Holy Grail of hockey before the start of the game. It was a glorious tribute to the iconic trophy, since between just those three players, they got to hold the Stanley Cup an incredible 23 times. (I'm not sure if it was planned by the event coordinator, but the tribute was still a nice touch since the Montreal Canadiens had won the Cup 23 times.)

Maurice Richard was given the honor of stepping out onto the ice first, flanked by "Le Gros Bill" and "Le demon blonde," but that first step was a little higher than Richard assumed and the 72-year-old tripped and dropped the Cup, putting a good-sized dent along its base. Richard quickly jumped to his feet, aided by Beliveau and Lafleur, and then they proceeded to parade around the Forum, holding the dented Cup above their heads like they did so many times in their careers.

Richard's stumble was a bad start to the 100th-year celebration, and the night got even stranger. The NHL All-Star game over the years had become a non-event. It was great to see the best players in the league at the time all on the same ice, but when the players put in only half effort, the event loses its purpose. The game was supposed to be for the fans, but recent All-Star games had left them with a sour taste in their mouths.

Bettman had just arrived in his new position, so he did not have enough time to make any changes to the format. The most exciting part of All-Star festivities was the skills competition. The 1993 All-Star Game was anything but a wondrous display of the NHL's top talents. The game was wide open, and players did not put in much of an effort. As a result, the Wales Conference had a 6–0 lead after the first period. The Campbell Conference did manage a few goals, but the game was a complete blowout by the Wales players, who ended the boring slaughter with a score of 16–6.

"I think the players wanted to make me feel comfortable. I came from a place [the NBA] where there was a lot of scoring," said Bettman to reporters after the game.

The NHL's premiere event was a farce, players failed to put in a good show and the product suffered, but Bettman had bigger issues to tackle in his first month on the job. A more pressing problem for the new commissioner to deal with was the issue of fighting in hockey. At the time, the hockey world and the sports beat writers were battling it out in the papers and on television over the role fighting played in hockey and the toll it takes on the players engaged in those battles—that is, the enforcers. The subject was on the minds of the hockey world because the summer before Bettman took over as commissioner, the NHL had lost tough guy John Kordic to a drug overdose. Now that Bettman was the leader of the league, the news media tried to probe the commissioner to find out where he stood on fighting in hockey.

Bettman, however, wanted to focus people's attention on the finer elements of the game and ordered up a bunch of slick new commercials. It was an effort to show the lighter side of hockey, marketing the game as a skilled sport and not the fight-filled matches that most non-hockey people thought of when asked about their impressions about the game. It proved to be a tough sell, since decades of popular culture had been branding the sport as violent. Movies like *Slap Shot* (1977), for example, did not help Bettman's cause, either.

The supporters of keeping fighting in hockey were worried about the new NHL boss and what he would do about the violence and the mounting public pressure to take it out of the game. The concerns were valid since Bettman was looking into expanding the NHL's influence in the United States, and it was genuinely feared that if the game was viewed as too violent, families would stay away from arenas in droves.

At the time, the debate was not only apparent in the media but also in the NHL boardrooms. In the spring of 1992, after some prompting by general managers, the league established a committee to study the positive and negative effects of fighting in hockey. After much study and reflection on the subject, the league put the committee's findings to a vote, and the majority of the hockey traditionalists rejected changes to the rules. The only change was a modification to the instigator rule, which said that if one player started a fight, he would be given an automatic game misconduct rather than a 10-minute penalty. The measures did not really help to stop fighting.

Reporters asked Bettman what his opinion was on fighting, and he gave a predictably political response: "I don't get particularly excited by fighting. Fighting doesn't turn me on, and it doesn't turn me off. I'd like to understand it better." He would get his chance to understand the complexities of allowing fighting in the game as he presided over his first season in the league. His first lesson might have been the Tie Domi trade to Winnipeg in 1992–93.

Those claiming the importance of fighting in the game and the role of the enforcer like to point to the case of Tie Domi and the Winnipeg Jets superstar rookie Teemu Selanne. When the Jets rookie started the 1992–93 season, he was on fire in the goal-scoring department, netting over 25 goals in his first 30 games in the league. But as his scoring went up, so did the amount of attention he was drawing from opposing teams that had no problem giving him a few extra whacks with their sticks.

As a result of the unwanted attention, Selanne's goal production began to slump. It was then that the Jets management decided to bring in some backup for the young sniper. Just before the New Year, Tie Domi was traded from the New York

Rangers to the Winnipeg Jets along with fellow enforcer Kris King, and in return, the Rangers got center Ed Olczyk. The moment Domi walked into the Jets dressing room, Selanne was the first to greet him with a big bear hug. In subsequent games after Domi's arrival in Winnipeg, Selanne's goal-scoring output was suddenly back on track, as any player who dared touch him was quickly regulated by Domi or King. Bettman would have to reconcile this aspect of using enforcers in the game, and the violence and fighting that often resulted, with an incident that happened during the 1993 playoffs.

In the opening round of the playoffs, the Patrick Division New York Islanders took on the Washington Capitals. The Islanders were a quick, puck-moving team led by their leading scorer Pierre Turgeon, while the Capitals had a more physical, defensive style of play led by big defenseman Al Iafrate and tough forward Dale Hunter. The two clubs had gotten well acquainted with each other during the regular season, so the division semifinal best-of-seven series promised to be entertaining.

It was a tight series, with Washington taking the first game by a score of 3–1. But the Islanders rallied on the strength of three straight overtime wins (two in double overtime) to take a 3–1 series lead and put the Capitals up against the ropes. Fortunately for the Capitals, they managed to pull off a 6–4 win at home to extend the series to game six, this time in New York.

Gary Bettman decided to show up to see what sparks would fly in the crucial game for both sides. Although the series had remained close, the New York Islanders completely and utterly dominated game six. By the middle of the third period, the Islanders were up 4–1. Barring a miracle, the Islanders had effectively ended the Capitals' hopes of lifting the Stanley Cup. The Islanders added insult to injury late in the third period.

The play started in the Capitals' zone when defenseman Al Iafrate shot the puck around the boards. It was picked up by veteran center Dale Hunter, who tried to flip the puck over to a team-mate, but the crafty leading scorer of the Island-ers, Pierre Turgeon, caught it. The Islanders' top scorer then swooped into the Capitals' zone, and with a crafty move, faked out goaltender Don Beaupre and put the puck into the net for the final nail in the Capitals' playoff coffin.

After scoring, Turgeon raised his arms into the air in pure elation. Two seconds later, Dale Hunter came from behind and sent him flying into the boards. When the melee was over, Turgeon lay on the ice in a daze, clutching his shoulder. He suffered a separated shoulder and had to miss several playoff games as a result.

Bettman, who was seated just a few rows away and had witnessed the hit, was disgusted by the cheap shot and reacted swiftly. Because this was the first major incident under his watch, he wanted to set the tone for his administration, and after reviewing the videotapes of the hit and taking into account Hunter's less-than-perfect past, he delivered the most severe punishment in NHL history. He handed the Capitals forward a 21-game suspension and a $150,000 fine.

"Under my watch, this is how I plan to deal with such incidents. If this isn't a suitable deterrent, I don't know what is," said Bettman to the media after the suspension announcement.

There was widespread praise for Bettman's quick and tough penalty, with many in the media claiming a new era in the NHL had been launched with Bettman's first and most public disciplining of a player. The early reviews of his decision seemed to favor the new commissioner.

The remainder of the playoffs continued without major incidents. Mario Lemieux gave a boost to the NHL public profile by returning to action in the division finals with his Pittsburgh Penguins taking on the New York Islanders. The excitement of the "Magnificent One" returning to the game was quickly extinguished by the Islanders' dramatic overtime defeat of the Penguins in game seven.

The playoffs, though, still held promise as both the Montreal Canadiens and the Toronto Maple Leafs made it through to the Conference finals. Canadians across the country were salivating at the idea of an all-Canadian final between the two iconic clubs that had not met in the finals since that fateful Maple Leafs Stanley Cup win in 1967. That was not to be, however, and Gary Bettman was likely happy about that because the game's other superstar, Wayne Gretzky, and his American-based Los Angeles Kings defeated the Maple Leafs to make it into the final against the Canadiens.

In the final series, the Montreal Canadiens came out victorious, while Gretzky had to return to his mansion in Los Angeles as a Stanley Cup loser, something he had experienced only one other time in his career (it would also be the last time he would make it into the Stanley Cup finals).

With the season put to bed, Bettman did not take a vacation or close down the head office as the league used to do in the past. He got to work and began the task of radically restructuring the office in the manner of a stereotypical lawyer—without emotion. Long-time employees that were stuck in the old system of the NHL were let go and replaced, and within months, the staff had doubled in size. To Bettman's way of thinking, for hockey to evolve, it had to change from the inside out. That summer, the new marketing department put together a campaign that tried to sell the sport as "the coolest game on earth." The slogan sounded like something Bettman came up with himself, but as cheesy as it was, it was effective.

The following season, Bettman's changes to the marketing, the structure of the league offices and the search for new business partners appeared to be working. The league was now finally moving up in the world of sports. The NHL posted record profits and added new teams, but more importantly, hockey as a product was becoming a valuable cultural commodity.

The video game developer Electronic Arts had a hit with its series of NHL games (*NHL 93* was my favorite), selling over one million copies. Snoop Dogg was seen wearing a Pittsburgh Penguins jersey and a Springfield Indians jersey of the American Hockey League in his incredibly popular song "Gin and Juice." Added to that was television's most popular sitcom *Friends*, which cast its characters Joey, Ross and Chandler as diehard

New York Rangers fans who often attended hockey games. Prior to these references to the game, the most exposure a hockey player ever received outside of Canada was Wayne Gretzky's appearance on *Saturday Night Live* in the summer of 1989 that spawned the supremely awful "Waikiki Hockey" skit.

In the early 1990s, peace and tranquility spread throughout the league. The owners were happy, the players seemed content, and the public, especially the American public, was in love with hockey. Then came the 1994 playoffs, which had everything Gary Bettman could have hoped for.

The new San Jose Sharks turned around their fortunes from their 1992–93 inaugural season—in which they won only 11 games—and made it into the playoffs. The upstart California club shocked the hockey world in the first round and defeated the seasoned Detroit Red Wings squad in a thrilling seven-game series, only to follow that up with another thriller in the Conference semifinals against the Toronto Maple Leafs that went all the way into a seventh game in which the Sharks were eliminated. Despite the elimination, the people of San Jose united behind their team and showed the rest of the hockey world that the game could survive and thrive in a southern market.

The playoffs received more marketable drama in the Eastern Conference as the New York Rangers went on a playoff run that rewrote their history. The Stanley Cup finals were set for May 27, 1994, after the New York Rangers spectacular victory over the New Jersey Devils. In that series, the hated Devils had taken a 3–2 lead and looked to finish off the Rangers on home ice. That was when talk of "the curse" surfaced.

The New York Rangers had been the toast of Broadway long ago, but time changes things, and the franchise had not won a championship since 1940. Despite coming close to winning the Stanley Cup on a few occasions, the Rangers faithful believed the team was cursed, and after 54 years, it appeared the hockey gods did not favor the Blueshirts. Many attribute the curse to Rangers' president John Reed Kilpatrick burning his fully paid mortgage deed in the bowl of Lord Stanley's Holy Grail when the Islanders won the Cup in 1940 against the Leafs. Some say this act was the cause of the Rangers 54-year Cup drought.

New York newspaper headlines reminded the Rangers that the curse had returned yet again. "It wasn't like you could avoid it," said Rangers forward Nick Kypreos about the supposed lore of the curse. "It was everywhere—in the newspapers, on TV, from the fans."

Rangers captain Mark Messier did not believe in curses and proclaimed in the locker room before the start of game six that the Rangers would win game six and game seven to advance into the finals. Messier's words seemed to fall on deaf ears in the opening minutes of game six as the Devils took a 2–0 lead, but the club reversed its luck and scored four straight unanswered goals (Messier with a hat trick) to win. The momentum carried over into game seven when the Rangers won a thriller in overtime to advance to the finals for the first time since 1979.

In the finals, the Rangers met the surprise Vancouver Canucks. It had all the promise of a classic series. A desperate Rangers team with a fan base dying for a Cup against a Canucks squad led by Russian superstar Pavel Bure. The Canucks had just managed to make the playoffs at the end of the regular season, and no one expected them to go far, but they defeated the Calgary Flames in a thrilling, game-seven double-overtime victory in the opening round. They then disposed of the Dallas Stars and the Toronto Maple Leafs in five games each.

The finals began with a 3–2 overtime win for the Canucks, and the New York papers, prone to exaggeration, cried that the curse would take the Rangers out once again, but the Blueshirts rallied to win the next three games to put the Vancouver Canucks on the edge. The Canucks won the next two games to force a game-seven Stanley Cup final but ran out of gas as the Rangers won the game 3–2 on a Messier Cup-clinching goal. All of New York breathed a sigh of relief as the curse had finally been lifted. It was the kind of Stanley Cup final that only comes along once in a while, and Bettman loved every second of it.

The 1994 playoffs had been played without much violence, and Bettman was soaking up most of the credit. The league appeared to have shed its image as a place for goons on skates, and it became a legitimate sport in the eyes of the rich American markets. During the summer of 1994, Bettman was walking around with his head held high. While the NHL was on the minds and lips of people everywhere, Bettman's old league, the NBA, was falling into disarray. Fights in the stands and on the court, as well as the sudden retirement of Michael Jordan, caused a huge drop in basketball revenue and TV ratings. You can be sure that Bettman got a chuckle out of the misfortunes of his former bosses.

The honeymoon period Gary Bettman was experiencing as the NHL's commissioner, though, did not last.

Chapter Four

Road to the First Lockout

Signs of discontent with Gary Bettman as NHL head administrator were present from the beginning of his appointment but were glossed over by his initial successes. For two Stanley Cup presentations in 1993 and 1994, no one in the stands booed the diminutive commissioner as he congratulated the winner, but that would soon change. Little by little, the ways in which the league would resolve its issues under Gary Bettman's leadership slowly began to materialize.

One of the first signs of trouble came when the NHL Officials Association's collective bargaining agreement came up for renewal at the end of the 1992–93 season. The association, led by player agent Don Meehan, negotiated with the league all summer throughout training camp with little progress being made. This was Bettman's first contract negotiations, and he did not want to appear soft on major issues. He took a hard stance and would not budge. The National Hockey League Officials Association (NHLOA) would not budge either, and by the start of the 1993–94 season, the two sides had still not come to an agreement. Seeing no signs of hope, members of the NHLOA met in Toronto in November 1993 and decided to go on strike.

Without officials, there is no hockey, so Bettman was forced to look for officials outside the NHL to ensure that the scheduled games could be played. There was just one issue. The NHL officials received support from officials in other spheres of hockey. Referees and linesmen from the Canadian Amateur Hockey Association (CAHA), USA Hockey, Major Junior Hockey, College Hockey and numerous minor professional hockey leagues rallied behind their striped brothers and refused to work any NHL games. This left the league with a huge problem, and it had to hire officials from leagues far and wide who really were not qualified to take over control of an NHL game. The results were not pretty.

The scab referees and linesmen did their best given the circumstances, but it just wasn't good enough. Flagrant missed calls, phantom offsides and overly harsh penalties abounded. Fans who had routinely booed the referees for calls against their team were now wanting them to come back.

The players and their union joined in the growing chorus of voices calling for the end to the officials' strike. After 17 painful days, Gary Bettman and his cadre of NHL negotiators were forced into an agreement that the NHLOA called "a new and improved Collective Bargaining Agreement." The enhancements in question were to the officials' severance pay, pension, retirement and playoff compensation.

It was a win for the Officials Association and one that the players paid close attention to, because behind the scenes, the NHLPA and Bettman were gearing up for their boardroom battle to come in the summer of 1994, when the NHLPA collective bargaining agreement came up for renegotiation. The new commissioner also had other headaches to deal with, as well as a few problems that he created himself.

In February 1993, the NHLPA failed in its attempt to strike a deal with the league to allow professional players to participate in the 1994 Winter Olympics in Lillehammer, Norway. Canadian fans and players alike were upset by the decision because they felt that if their best players were allowed to enter the tournament, they would finally have a chance at gold in hockey, a medal Canada had not won since 1952.

Toronto Maple Leafs forward Glen Anderson had foreseen the league banning the players from the Olympics and had purposely put a clause in his contract with the Leafs that permitted him to leave the team for two weeks and help the Canadian national team. The Leafs enthusiastically supported Anderson's decision, but the NHL head office had final approval. Gary Bettman, who was never one to break a rule, referred to the rulebook, which stated that only players with less than a year of professional experience were permitted to leave the NHL to play for Team Canada. Bettman was hoping the issue would end there, as the regulations were quite clear, but when it comes to hockey, people's passions often make them overlook the rules.

Shortly after it was announced that the players, and more specifically Glen Anderson, were not permitted to attend the Olympics, a young girl named Tiffany Williams, who just happened to be a huge Glen Anderson fan, took up the cause and started a petition to get Bettman to reconsider his stance on the Olympics. In a few weeks, the determined 11-year-old had more than 6000 signatures.

Showing some media savvy, Tiffany took her cause to flamboyant member of Parliament John Nunziata, who could not pass up the political capital and imagery of a little girl and her quest for the sake of hockey. Nunziata immediately set up a meeting with Bettman in New York, and Nunziata and Tiffany flew down for a closed-door meeting.

While a throng of Canadian media waited outside the NHL boardroom, Bettman listened to Nunziata's and Tiffany's arguments. Two hours later, Tiffany emerged from the boardroom looking sad and defeated. Nunziata puffed out his chest for the cameras and exclaimed, "It's clear to me he's just a little dictator." In hindsight, one has to wonder at the logic of Bettman agreeing to the meeting, as the media firestorm that followed certainly did not help the new commissioner's public persona.

Bettman's relations with the players also took a hit early on in his administration. Nearing the end of the 1993–94 season, the NHLPA tried to negotiate a deal with the league to share a piece of the lucrative merchandising revenue it received from placing players' names on the backs of jerseys. The players deemed it only fair since their names were being used to sell the jerseys. But Bettman delayed making a decision, so the players decided to play hardball and tried to cut their own deal with the merchandise vendors. Bettman was furious at the backhanded move and personally served Mike Gartner, the NHLPA president, with legal papers to stop the NHLPA deal, just before a game. People were fast learning that when it came to business, Bettman did not play games.

The players knew what to expect when Bettman was hired. They had seen the installation of a salary cap in the NBA and Bettman's role in strong-arming the players into accepting it. The first salvo in the upcoming collective bargaining renegotiations started near the end of the 1993–94 season. Bettman put together a proposal he figured was fair, but he had to know that it would be rejected. He suggested that the league set up a sort of trickle-down offer in which the league would "set" each team's payroll, then let the players divide the excess that fell from the top. The NHLPA took one look at the deal and rejected it without so much as asking its members to review the details.

More talks and more negotiations followed during the spring and into the summer of 1994, but the NHLPA still judged the offers to be insulting. Bettman, however, saw a trend in the league that was leading to financial instability. In 1990, the average player was making in the area of $250,000, with only four players earning over the magical million-dollar mark: Wayne Gretzky, Mario Lemieux, Mark Messier and Steve Yzerman. But as the decade progressed, some of the owners were shooting themselves in the foot by beginning to sign lesser stars to multi-year, multimillion-dollar contracts. The team owners, however, no longer had their best friend, player agent Alan Eagleson, behind the scenes of the NHLPA cooking the books and convincing the players with his forked tongue that their low-paying salaries and perks were enough. Now the league was flooded with new agents, businessmen who, in most cases, knew the art of negotiation and business better than the owners.

Bettman was brought in to bring the ridiculous spending under control and tighten rules so rogue owners did not put their team's financial success over the league's well-being. Bettman also wanted to completely scale back spending, but the players were not buying into his logic. On top of implementing the dreaded salary-cap system, Bettman and the owners were also seeking to reduce rookie salaries, scrap the arbitration system and lower the playoff bonuses the players had gained during the last deal with John Ziegler. All of these items were a part of the negotiating agreement, but as training camp neared, Bettman dropped a bomb on the players, one that turned the whole process into a bitter, nasty struggle.

In August 1994, Bettman basically told the NHLPA that he was removing the players' perks and benefits when the existing contract expired in September. The tactic was meant to put pressure on the players to sign a deal, but the players instantly saw it as a slap in the face. The removal of the "perks" meant that players were still welcome to go to training camp, but they would have to pay for their own flights to get there, as well as pay extra costs, such as insurance and meals. The players were none too happy, and the most vocally upset was Chris Chelios, who held absolutely nothing back when expressing his opinions on the subject of the lockout and Gary Bettman.

"He's going to affect a lot of people, and some crazed fan—or maybe even a player, who knows— is going to take things into their own hands. And figure they're going to get him out of the way and maybe things will get settled. You'd hate to see something like that happen, but he took the job," said the veteran defenseman, completely unafraid to speak his mind.

Although harsh, Chelios' words spoke to the developing climate as the start of the 1994–95 season approached. Soon, other players were speaking up in their own ways. Some were seen sporting NHLPA baseball caps, and Montreal Canadiens defenseman Mathieu Schneider plastered the words "Bettman Sucks" on his helmet during practice. Even the face of hockey, the "Great One" himself, spoke up on league affairs, not mincing his words: "I've played this game for thirty years, and for someone to come along who has only been in our sport for one year and tell us that we're not going to play is very frustrating and extremely disappointing."

In the old days of league/player negotiations, the process had been relatively smooth. Alan Eagleson, the team owners and the NHL president had crafted deals behind players' backs, so negotiations always went according to what the owners and the league wanted, and the players were left none the wiser. But when Eagleson was fired and eventually convicted of stealing money from the players' union (among other offenses), the players finally awoke to the reality of the NHL and began demanding their fair share. They were unwilling to put up with a status quo that was skewed in favor of the owners and the league. The players were ready to take on the league and the owners because they had their own pit bull to back them up now.

Bob Goodenow, executive director of the NHLPA (1992–2005), was Bettman's arch-nemesis. They battled within the shadows of the boardroom, walked the line between good and evil and played with the lives of others. Ying to yang, fire to water, the two heads of their organizations were pretty much at constant odds at the table.

Goodenow was exactly the type of executive director the NHLPA needed at the time. He had a background in hockey, having played during his college days at Harvard and gotten as far as the International Hockey League's Flint Generals before giving up his hockey career to focus on his law degree (with a specialization in labor relations). After a few years of practicing law in the everyday business world of unions and politicians, he started out his path in the NHL as a player agent, making himself and his most famous client, Brett Hull, millionaires. The players trusted a man who knew the pressures of playing the game and who had once sought a life in the big leagues. They handed over the reins to Goodenow after Eagleson's departure, and Goodenow set about refurbishing the NHLPA brand.

He moved the NHLPA from his own existing offices to a brand-new space devoted entirely to the association's business. He also hired a handful of employees and began turning the institution into a respectable opponent against the league.

Goodenow's first order of business was to ask the players to start putting some money aside because he knew what the future would bring.

The NHLPA emergency coffers had run dry under Eagleson, so Goodenow had no extra funds in case of a strike or lockout, so the players would have to fend for themselves during the next battle with the league.

That battle came about soon after Goodenow took over. In the spring of 1992, he set the NHLPA into its first players' strike. He proved to be an excellent negotiator, getting the players a much needed boost in revenues and gaining negotiation rights during individual contract negotiations for players. He so deftly handled John Ziegler that the owners fired the league boss before the ink could dry on his contract.

Then Gary Bettman arrived in town. I imagine their first meeting to be like an Old West showdown. Eyes locked beneath the glare of florescent office lights, a tense quiet in the air with the faint sound of briefcases opening, then *bam!*, out come the contracts and legal briefs that get sprayed all over the room.

The reality, though, is that the moment Bettman took over the job of NHL commissioner , he arranged several informal meetings with Goodenow during games or over dinners to try to create some sort of common tolerance for each other. After all, they were both Ivy League guys who had studied labor relations—what couldn't they have in common?

The idea of them becoming friends, however, would be like a college nerd and a college jock becoming drinking buddies. (I'll let you guess which one was the nerd and which the jock.) Bettman's attempt at forging a good working relationship was valiant, but Goodenow had to keep his distance. The players were watching him carefully to see if he showed any kind of rapport that might give them cause to doubt his commitment to the their side. This was a cold war between two men with similar characters, both strong in their opinions and both unwilling to bend. Negotiations were about to get prickly.

Bettman and the team owners were the first to make a move. They presented their case that the league was in trouble and that some teams were losing millions of dollars a year while a few others were making only a buck. Bettman claimed that teams like the expansion Florida Panthers and the Quebec Nordiques were millions of dollars in the red, and that if the financial stability of the league was not established, there might not be an NHL in the future.

Goodenow stood firm and publicly called the NHL's claims "creative accounting," and he produced his own set of figures. He claimed the league had achieved record profits and had just penned a lucrative television distribution deal with the Fox Network. Plus, it wasn't like the owners were holding back their money; they were signing more and more players to never-before-seen sums of money per year.

The two sides battled back and forth well into training camp, then the pre-season schedule, and eventually the games began falling off the calendar. October passed with no resolution, then November, and both sides were still firmly entrenched. The NHL tried every dirty trick in the book to get the players to break their stance, including giving press conferences that denounced the executive of the NHLPA and sending out documents of the league's latest offers in the hopes of dividing and conquering the players from within.

Words and slogans were lobbed from both sides, including accusations of each being anti-American, anti-Canadian, anti-Semitic, against the fans and in it only for the money. The battle went on in the media for months, leaving fans shaking their heads in frustration while waiting for some movement so that the season could start.

All the while, the league and the players were collectively losing millions of dollars. As the days turned into weeks, and then months, nerves began to wear thin, and even the normally cool-headed Bettman began to show signs of tiring. During one meeting with the NHLPA, he even went as far as screaming obscenities about his equal on the other side of the boardroom and stomping out of the meeting, like a child denied his favorite toy at the store.

Bettman's behavior was completely uncharacteristic and was an isolated incident. He preferred a more subtle method of letting his negotiating opponents know that he didn't like them, subtle but obvious. It is what angers people about Bettman. I am sure a lot of people would rather see the angry Bettman over the cold snake that he comes across as most of the time. For example, during the negotiations, he consistently referred to the players as "labor." Bettman's choice of words spoke to a certain lack of respect for the players, the institution of hockey and was a sneaky, underhanded slap in the face.

In late November, some progress was made when the players conceded on a few issues pertaining to salaries, but the offer was flatly rejected by the owners because they wanted more concessions from the association. Then in December, with nothing moving, the league announced the cancellation of the All-Star Game.

It seemed to everyone watching and involved that this was heading in only one direction. Some players left North America to earn a decent paycheck in the European leagues, while others opened up a business or worked in an existing business they were partnered in. Late into the month, some players were even whispering to reporters that they wished the whole thing was behind them and that Goodenow would just sign the next contract offer.

The big bad owners were also starting to waver in the face of the mounting lost revenues and were quietly urging Bettman to end the affair. The pressure was building, and there was the real possibility that the season would be cancelled and that the Stanley Cup would not be handed out—something that hadn't happened since the 1919 Spanish flu pandemic forced the cancellation of the playoffs. See Appendices for more information.

The players were dead set against agreeing to a salary cap, and the league finally relented from its cap requirements. After the Christmas break, it seemed time away from the boardroom and spending time with loved ones helped to calm attitudes. However, there still was a long way to go. Bettman had circled January 10, 1995, as the end date of negotiating. If that day came and went with no agreement between the two sides, the season would have to be cancelled.

It was left in the hands of Bettman and Goodenow to hammer out the details. Bettman knew that if they failed to come to an agreement, the blame for the loss of the season would be placed squarely on his shoulders since he had been the one who made the decision to lockout the "labor."

It wasn't until January 9 that the two sides sat down for a make or break session. The meeting started at 10:00 AM, and by 7:00 PM the next day, a deal had been signed. The players agreed to a salary cap for rookies at USD$850,000. The arbitration system would continue, but the owners would get a few more rights in the process, and an agreement was made on the age of free agency. The contract was signed for a six-year period, with options to reopen talks at the end of the 1997–98 season. After 103 days with no hockey, it was announced that the game would return but with a shortened schedule of 48 games.

Who were the winners and who were the losers? It's hard to choose in this case. The league felt they came out of the negotiations smelling like roses, having got a cap on rookie salaries, and they also got better negotiating rights in arbitration. The players felt they did a good job of avoiding the salary cap for most players, and they also got a few concessions in free agency and player perks.

Gary Bettman, the mouthpiece of the NHL and the owners, came out a clear loser. Despite being hired to do the bidding of the league, he became the scapegoat for the growing discontent within the hockey world and especially among the fans. Things would only get worse for Bettman as the years went on.

Chapter Five

In Between Lockouts

With the lockout behind him, and the NHL Collective Bargaining Agreement (CBA) set in stone until 1997, Gary Bettman got back to the business of running the league. After all the nastiness that occurred during the CBA negotiations, he was just as happy as the rest of the hockey world to once again watch the best players on the globe play the greatest game on earth.

The 1994–95 season was a strange one. The last time the NHL played a 48-game schedule, Bryan Hextall of the New York Rangers led the league in scoring, Boston's Frank Brimsek was the leading goaltender and the Toronto Maple Leafs were crowned 1941–42 Stanley Cup champions. But however odd it was, once the players hit the ice, it was back to business as usual.

Jaromir Jagr took over the top spot as leading scorer—the first time someone not named Wayne

Gretzky or Mario Lemieux had won the scoring title since 1979–80. Gretzky was starting to show signs of slowing down, finishing the season with 48 points, while Lemieux sat out the entire season because of the lingering effects of back injuries and his battle with cancer. The Quebec Nordiques, Pittsburgh Penguins, Philadelphia Flyers, Calgary Flames and Detroit Red Wings were the top teams in the league going into the playoffs.

The Detroit Red Wings, winners of the President's Trophy, did not surprise anyone by beating Dallas, San Jose and Chicago en route to the Stanley Cup final. In the Eastern Conference, the New Jersey Devils, led by a young goaltender named Martin Brodeur, played a shutdown defensive style of hockey—the infamous "neutral zone trap" that stymied Boston, Pittsburgh and the Flyers—to put the Devils into the finals for the first time in their franchise's history.

The Detroit Red Wings, led by Steve Yzerman, Sergei Fedorov and Dino Ciccarelli, were the third highest scoring team in the regular season and loved to play a fast, exciting game. The New Jersey Devils were the complete opposite. With head coach Jacques Lemaire at the helm, the Devils had a solid lineup of good hockey players, but none could compare with the likes of Steve Yzerman or Sergei Fedorov in terms of scoring. The Devils had the tough players, the grinders, the fighters, the pests and the forecheckers, all guys willing to do the dirty work but not many of whom could finish off a play and score the all-important goals.

The highest scorer on the Devils that season was Stephane Richer, who scored 23 goals and 16 assists. The next highest goal scorers had 17 goals, another had 12 and two more players had 10 goals; no one else on their team had goals in the double digits. But what the Devils did have was a system. Jacques Lemaire recognized his team's weakness and implemented a defensive system to allow his players to compete against top clubs. Called the "neutral zone trap," the system functions by clogging up the neutral zone when the opposing team starts moving up the ice. This meant it was next to impossible for teams to start rushes up ice to establish a presence in the New Jersey zone. To do so, the opposing team had to dump the puck in and hope they could out-muscle a team of grinders and checkers. After that, if the opposing team managed to pick up the puck, they still had to get it by Martin Brodeur, which wasn't easy.

The system made the Devils competitive, but the games could be downright boring and low scoring. A New Jersey Devils game usually started out with the Devils scoring one or two goals, then they would tighten up the game with a heavy presence in the neutral zone and win the game by a score of 2–1. The team's total goals for and against proves the point. During the 1994–95 season, the team scored a total of 136 goals while they had 121 goals scored against them. The Detroit Red Wings, in comparison, scored 180 goals while only allowing 117 against them.

Going into the finals, the Red Wings seemed like the only team capable of breaking the Devils' suffocating style of play with their talent and speed, but during the first period of the first game, it was evident that even the Red Wings did not have an answer to Lemaire's system. The Devils potted two goals and then clamped down on defense, allowing only one Red Wing goal. The pattern continued into games two, three and four, with the Devils blocking the Red Wings at every turn. The system worked, however frustrating it was for fans to watch, and the Devils won their franchise's first Stanley Cup.

After handing out two previous Stanley Cups to polite applause, this time around, Gary Bettman was welcomed to the ice in New Jersey by a chorus of boos from the fans as he introduced the Conn Smythe winner, Claude Lemieux. He was again booed in his preamble to handing over the Stanley Cup to Devils' captain Scott Stevens. It was Bettman's first real taste of booing from the fans for his part in the lockout, and it would not be his last.

The finish of the 1994–95 regular season brought the end of an era in Quebec City. The demise of the Quebec Nordiques in Quebec City started with the league's request to house the team in a new building. The Colisée de Quebec was built in 1949 for the Quebec Aces of the American Hockey League and was never meant to be the home of an NHL club, but when the Nordiques arrived on the scene in 1979–80, the arena was sufficient for the fledgling pro team. However, by 1995, as teams around the league were moving into new arenas or still in the planning stages of building new ones, the City of Quebec had no plans for a new arena, and any talk of building one led to many arguments.

The ownership group of the Nordiques, led by Marcel Aubut, tried to pressure the city and the province to pay for the construction of a new building. If they wouldn't pay, Aubut threatened to move the team elsewhere. He knew his demands would get no traction in Quebec as he doubled down on his demands by asking taxpayers to also cover the team's losses during the entire construction phase.

Aubut had hoped that the recent resurgence of the young team in the league standings would help his cause in getting a new arena. However, at the time, the province of Quebec was focused on the 1995 sovereignty referendum and had no interest in saving a hockey team. Despite the climate of uncertainty, it seemed unlikely to the fans and the players that the team would fold operations and head out of town. When the Nordiques bowed out of the first round of the playoffs on May 16, 1995, few thought the club would not be there the following season. But behind the scenes, things were looking more and more grim.

Before the month was out, Aubut met with the provincial and city governments one last time to hammer out a deal on constructing a new arena. The governments' final offer was several millions of dollars short of what Aubut thought was sufficient, so on May 24, 1995, Aubut signed a deal with Comcast Entertainment Group for USD$75 million, effectively moving the Quebec Nordiques out of Canada and into Denver, Colorado. The Nordiques were now the Colorado Avalanche.

In public, Aubut said that he was trying to save the team, but behind closed doors, he knew that the team was doomed by the time the lockout ended. The month-to-month losses by the team were just too much to bear. Gary Bettman later revealed in a 2009 court battle related to the Phoenix Coyotes that it had taken months for the 1995 Denver–Quebec deal to be put together: "We knew very early on, in the middle of that season at the latest, that this franchise was likely to be moved. [Aubut] spent something like two or three months living in my office. He actually had an office in the office, where he was working on the sale."

After the announcement, hatred toward Bettman ramped up across Canada, mostly because several other Canadian franchises were also on shaky financial ground. The Edmonton Oilers, the Ottawa Senators and the Winnipeg Jets were barely surviving in the current NHL market, and with the recent push to build newer arenas, it looked like they might all fold.

To make matters worse for fans of Canadian hockey, the Colorado Avalanche had an incredible 1995–96 season. Getting star goaltender Patrick Roy really helped the club overall. The Avalanche took the momentum of the season into the play-offs and ended up winning the Stanley Cup. Although previous Nordiques fans were happy for their former club, they were also extremely bitter at the missed opportunity to celebrate a Cup in the Old City of Quebec.

While Quebec was in mourning, the hockey fans in Winnipeg were freaking out. Seeing the demise of the Nordiques pushed the fans to try harder to keep the Jets, but the powers that be who were dealing with the reality of the Winnipeg Jets' future in Canada had a much more difficult time staying positive.

The realities of the new NHL were hitting the smaller clubs in the pocketbook. As the league opened up new clubs south of the border, the small Canadian markets could not keep up. Operating costs were rising, as were players' salaries and expenses. Teams earning money in the low Canadian dollar were at a significant disadvantage when they had to pay salaries to the players in American currency. (At the time, the exchange rate was USD$1.40 to CDN$1.00.) It didn't help that the richer American teams, such as the free-spending New York Rangers, the Los Angeles Kings and the Pittsburgh Penguins, were driving up player costs by offering their stars huge contracts that none of the smaller Canadian clubs could hope to compete or even keep up with.

Clubs like Winnipeg and the Nordiques received plenty of moral support from the government, but when the teams came knocking on the provincial capital and federal doors with their hands out for millions of dollars to build new arenas, the governments went silent.

The move to a more southern climate had already been established when the Minnesota

North Stars packed their bags and headed to Texas to become the Dallas Stars after the 1992–93 season. Overnight, that franchise went from a small-market team barely able to get by to a multimillion-dollar organization. The league did not fight particularly hard to prevent teams from moving to other cities, so the outlook for the small-market Canadian teams was not good.

It was difficult for the average fan to reconcile the sold-out crowds with a failing franchise while other teams in the U.S. struggled to put fans in the seats. Winnipeg fans were some of the most loyal and obsessed in the league and spent a good deal of money on their team to show that support, but it just wasn't enough. To save the team and stop it from going the way of the Nordiques, the Jets needed a savior.

The owner of the Jets as of 1995, Barry Shenkarow had been keeping an eye out for a new owner since the end of the lockout. However, as the 1994–95 season came to a close, with the Jets out of a playoff spot, it looked like all hopes had been lost to find someone to keep the team in Winnipeg. The drive to save the Jets spread throughout the city in the early months of 1995. The first to step up with an offer to purchase the team was a consortium of around 70 local business leaders. The group had put forth an offer of

$32 million for the team and a promise to build a $120-million arena with the help of three levels of government. Several members of the consortium met at Winnipeg mayor Susan Thompson's office for a conference call with the NHL commissioner. However, after the group finished detailing their plan to Bettman, the other end of the line went quiet. When Bettman did speak, he said their offer was unrealistic given that the league was getting more expensive to operate. He then announced the most important factor to the deal he wanted: there had to be a primary owner, and that if they wanted to sell the team before the year 2000, a $50-million transfer fee had to be paid.

Bettman's comments took the consortium by complete surprise, and the group's members did everything in their power not to throw the phone out the mayor's office window. After they hung up, they had a heated discussion about Bettman's proposal. Let's just say that nice things were not said about the commissioner.

The consortium called Bettman back and gave him an earful about changing directions so suddenly and said there was no way to meet his demands. Throughout the conversation, Bettman remained his quiet, reserved self, but to the people on the other end of the phone, he came across as being purely smug.

The mayor and some of the local business leaders exited her office into the throng of eagerly awaiting Winnipeg journalists. Her demeanor when the mayor addressed the media did not bode well for the future of the Jets. Thompson and the members of the consortium did not hold back in their contempt for the commissioner, calling his tactics underhanded. They indicated that Bettman didn't seem willing to accept any offer they proposed. It was apparent to them that Bettman made up his mind long ago to move the Winnipeg Jets to the highest bidder.

The following day, Jets fans awoke to the news that their beloved team was only two steps from leaving the city for good. Bettman became enemy number one in the province of Manitoba, and the louder that the fans screamed, the more the press picked up the story. It was a public relations nightmare. All across Canada and in the smaller markets of the NHL, Bettman was vilified. His image as the cold businessman had now turned into the cold American trying to steal the game away from Canada.

To try to calm the growing furor, which had even reached the ears of then Prime Minister Jean Chretien, Bettman decided to fly to Winnipeg to listen to the concerns of the city and the consortium just before the start of the 1995 playoffs. Under police escort, Bettman arrived for the meeting with Mayor Susan Thompson and the group trying to buy the Jets. It seemed that Bettman had learned nothing from his impromptu meeting a few years earlier with the little girl who wanted Glen Anderson to play in the Olympics. Bettman sat in a boardroom and listened to the buyers' pitch, but he was not swayed. Not one person on the other side of the table could say anything positive about Bettman, calling his tone "arrogant" and his manner "robotic."

For Bettman, it was all still just the name of the game, business. After the meeting, Bettman and Jets' owner Barry Shenkarow addressed the press. Bettman responded in a typical lawyerly way. "It's too easy to pick on me because I'm an American," he said, referring to a Friday demonstration that had targeted him. "If you want to do it, go ahead. But it's not accurate. I'm not the one who created the situation. I'm trying to deal with it." Then Bettman reiterated that he was committed to keeping hockey franchises in Canada, but that the teams had to be economically viable in order to justify their existence. It was then that he pushed the knife in a little deeper into the hopes of Jets' fans. "This is not an NHL decision. This is really up to the people in Winnipeg and the prospective owners...to see if there's something to be done to keep the team there," Bettman said. "But the biggest problem is there doesn't seem to be anybody, in a serious fashion, who wants to own the franchise."

It was an open casting call for prospective owners, but no one showed up. The Jets' fate was sealed. Near the middle of May 1995, Shenkarow began fielding offers and soon had a few bites. To add insult to injury, the sale of the team could not be concluded in time, and the Jets would have one last season in the NHL before the sword of Damocles fell from above and killed the once beloved hockey club.

The 1995–96 season was an odd one for Winnipeg Jets fans. Although nothing could be done to stop the sale of the club by the time the season got underway, the slightest flicker of hope remained. Every news story and every rumor of keeping the team in Winnipeg was followed, but each one led to a dead-end. The final game for the Winnipeg Jets took place on April 28, 1996, in game six of the Conference quarterfinals against the Detroit Red Wings. The Red Wings had just eliminated the Jets with a 4–1 win. Defenseman Norm Maciver scored the final goal of the original Jets' franchise. The clock had run out on the city and its hopes of a Stanley Cup champion. Every single person at the final game cheered, but it was sad applause, and everyone in that arena that night knew that Bettman was the one to blame, right or wrong.

Journalist Jeffery Simpson wrote an editorial in the *Globe and Mail* that summed up the over-whelming sentiment across Canada after the announcement of the sale of the Jets: "Now only a requiem remains for professional hockey in Winnipeg, and quite probably for other Canadian cities in the years ahead. The critical mass of Canadian teams is declining, and will decline further. The Canadian influence in our 'national game' is waning. The Winnipeg Jets' demise is but one example of this trend." Simpson also added, "Once the new labor agreement with the players was signed without any revenue-sharing and only a modest series of restraints on salaries, the Jets' fate was probably sealed."

And it was. During the 1995–96 regular season, the people of Winnipeg had learned that Barry Shenkarow and Gary Bettman had agreed to the sale of the franchise to businessmen Steve Glukstern and Richard Burke, who wanted to move a franchise back into Minnesota, the city that had lost their North Stars just three years earlier. The outrage and hatred for Bettman grew to epic proportions after this little bit of news was announced.

It seemed Bettman had simply removed one small-market team in Canada and replaced it with another small-market American team in a city that had failed to support their former franchise just a few years back. But when the deal to place the team in Minnesota fell through, Gluckstern and Burke partnered with Phoenix-based businessman Jerry Colangelo to officially make the Winnipeg Jets the Phoenix Coyotes for the start of the 1996–97 season.

The realignment of the league, though, was not over. The low Canadian dollar was causing problems for the Canadian teams still left in the league. Despite all the negative press directed at Gary Bettman by Canadian hockey fans, he knew that the league could not survive without Canada. The country contains the spiritual heart of the game and has supported hockey through darker times in the past without question. Although Bettman was crucified in the Canadian media for his handling of the Winnipeg Jets, little praise was given when, before the lockout, he was forced to step in between Oilers' owner Peter Pocklington and his desire to move the Oilers out of Edmonton.

Bettman had stopped Pocklington from selling off the Oilers in order to secure funds to repair Edmonton's aging arena. Immediately after the lockout, though, Pocklington was back in the media crying about the mounting costs to run the Oilers. The people of Edmonton rallied around their team, but they needed to go the extra mile to keep their team in the city. Besides Edmonton, both Ottawa and Calgary were also facing an uncertain future. The situation became so dire for the clubs that Bettman had to persuade the NHL board of governors to do something to ensure that hockey remained in Canada.

When talk of revenue sharing among teams had come up in the past, the majority of the team owners had squashed the idea flat out. But by December 1995, Bettman managed to sway them, saying that it was the only way to keep the league at status quo, at least for a few years until another solution could be found. The NHL had already moved out two Canadian clubs and might face a revolution should another one leave.

The board agreed with Bettman and allowed a revenue-sharing program to go into effect, where a small percentage of funds would be taken from the top clubs and redistributed among the smaller clubs at the bottom. To gain entry into the revenue-sharing program, though, the struggling clubs had to guarantee the sale of at least 13,000 season tickets by a certain date. The Oilers fan base stood up and barely made the quota, with 13,482 tickets sold. Ottawa and Calgary managed to secure emergency funding to stay afloat.

The revenue-sharing program, however, was only a temporary solution. The late 1990s were not good years for Gary Bettman. He did secure a few successes, but they were completely overshadowed by his failures. He had been brought into the league to help fix what was broken, and given that much of the league was in bad need of repair, Bettman was given powers to basically make alterations wherever he saw fit. Naturally, this meant transforming the financial, legal and administrative functions of the league, but Bettman was given even more powers. He was allowed to tinker with the way the game was played on the ice and consumed by the public.

One of the first visible changes he made was related to the way the game was viewed on television. It was supposed to make hockey-newbies excited and less confused, while hockey purists did not know whether to laugh and scream bloody heresy. Gary Bettman's goal was to introduce hockey to as many people as he could. Throughout most of the United States, hockey was lost in a sea of flashy, basketball marketing giants like Michael Jordan and all the hype of Super Bowl Sundays.

If you had asked any random American man what came to his mind when he thought of hockey, most would say nothing, some would know a few facts or maybe mention Gretzky's name. Even fewer would be able to carry on a conversation about what the Leafs chances would be that year (terrible). Hockey to a lot of Americans originated from a place where players put on skates and beat themselves. It was that sport that Paul Newman played in that movie only Canadians love. Hockey had an image problem.

If Bettman wanted new fans to pour into the new franchises he wanted to open, he would have to teach the uninitiated about hockey—from scratch. The education process took place through the use of marketing, but Bettman needed something else to help people follow the game in real time on television. Hockey had been followed on television by millions of people for decades without much complaint, but Bettman thought there was a genuine problem when dealing with the new American audience—a problem big enough that he needed to try something completely different and unexpected.

Granted, the NHL needed to do something to attract more fans, but hockey was and is a sport filled with ardent traditionalists. Change was something that happened very slowly. It took a man like Gary Bettman to break with traditions. He wanted to help those new audiences in Tampa Bay, Miami, San Jose and Dallas discover the game and learn its complexities as fast as they could. When Fox signed on to broadcast the NHL games, the network packaged the game differently and approached each break in play as an opportune moment to explain to the viewing audience what was happening on the ice and why. But in that first year, the biggest complaint the Fox executive heard from TV viewers was that they had trouble following the game and "that darn tiny black disk." So a bunch of NHL and Fox executives got together in a room and came up with a few ideas that were presented to a series of focus groups. What came out of that idea grinder was something lovingly titled, "The FoxTrax Puck."

The FoxTrax Puck was basically a regular, vulcanized rubber puck spilt in half, then filled with a ton of technology that made the puck magically appear in brilliant colors so that you could easily follow it on your TV screen. The batteries that powered the puck were designed to last for around 30 minutes, but often the time ended up being just 10 minutes. The infrared and shock sensors in the puck relayed information back to the cameras that would then translate the puck's movements on screen into a bluish glow around the puck. When a player hit the puck, a bluish comet tail would light up onscreen indicating the puck's trajectory, and as an added feature, when the puck traveled faster than 70 miles per hour, a red comet tail appeared behind the puck, clearly showing where the puck was onscreen. Problem solved, right?

Reactions to the "glo-puck," as people were calling it, were mixed. American audiences welcomed the addition with open arms, saying that it helped them follow the game. However, hockey purists (Canadians and pockets of a few thousand fans scattered across the United States, mainly within influential distance from the Canadian border) were not happy with the comet tails and bluish glow on their TV screens; they complained that the new technology made their blessed game look like a cartoon. They didn't see the problem in following a black puck on a white sheet of ice. How hard could it be?

Despite the detractors, the Fox Network kept the glow puck until the end of the 1998 Stanley Cup finals. The following season, the U.S. NHL broadcast contract expired with Fox, and ABC took over translating the game for Americans. Hockey purists everywhere breathed a collective sigh of relief. The FoxTrax Puck was bad, yes, but some liked the concept, and Bettman had been willing to try something new to sell the game. His already damaged hockey street-cred, though, had been tarnished even further.

There was also a problem with the game itself. It started to slow down, scoring dropped off significantly and fans began yawning in their seats. You can easily point to a lot of reasons why the game had changed: the effects of expansion allowed more lower-quality players into the league, thereby diluting the talent pool per team; lax officiating in calling hooking penalties; and the trap system popularized by the New Jersey Devils was now spreading to other clubs trying to make their way to the top without the necessary talent to do so.

The league that once spawned Gretzky's incredible scoring streaks, Mario Lemieux's dazzling skills on the ice and the rookie sensations of Jaromir Jagr and Teemu Selanne now had these players struggling to score close to 100 points in a full season in 1997–98, when it took Gretzky only half a season to get 100 points in 1981–82. At the end of the 1997–98 season, only Jaromir Jagr of the Penguins had broken the 100-point mark, with a total of 102 points, and just three other players were in the 90-point range. When Bettman took over control in 1992–93, 20 players finished the season with over 100 points, with Mario Lemieux leading the way with 160 points and Teemu Selanne and Alexander Mogliny scoring a league-leading 76 goals. It wasn't just the forwards and the defensemen that were changing in the new Bettman-led league. The goaltenders were getting better, too.

The same year that Teemu scored his 76 goals and Lemieux tallied 160 points, the Vezina-winning goaltender that season, Ed Belfour, finished the regular season with a goals-against average of 2.59 in 71 games played. By 1997–98, Belfour had improved to a goals-against of 1.88 in 61 games played. The same statistical improvement happened to all the top goaltenders across the league. Martin Brodeur dropped close to a full percentage point in goals-against from his rookie-year performance of 2.40 in 1993–94 to 1.88 in 1997–98. Even Ron Tugnutt, a career backup goaltender for the most part, dropped his goals-against average to incredible lows, from 3.16 in 1993–94 to 1.79 in 1998–99.

The gist of all this was that something in hockey had changed. The goaltenders were getting better. Goaltending had become a science. Since the percentages had the majority of shots on goal coming into the lower half of the net, goalie coaches everywhere were teaching up-and-comers the butterfly style. This stance led to a decrease in goal scoring, but the new goaltending technique wasn't the only reason.

Anyone who watched hockey prior to about 1995 must surely have noticed that goaltenders across the league seemed to be growing in size. This was not because general managers were recruiting larger players, but because many goaltenders were wearing equipment that belied the tiny frames underneath their jerseys. For comparison, take a look at goaltenders from the 1980s, then look at the mid-1990s. It would appear you are comparing a teenager to a full-grown man. The most obvious example of the change of goalie size was Patrick Roy in the mid to late 1990s. In the 1993 run to the Stanley Cup, he wore reasonable-sized padding that fit his frame, but by the time he joined the Colorado Avalanche in 1995, Roy had either gained a lot of weight since 1993 or he had been playing with his equipment.

The goaltenders expanded in all directions. Their catching and blocking gloves grew, their body armor made them look like sumo wrestlers, and the leg pads looked like floatation devices. Although the rulebook stated the official size limitations of goalie padding, the equipment managers at the time were getting more creative in the application of the rules. The league eventually cracked down, but goalie equipment was another factor in the drop in goal scoring.

The goaltenders were also receiving much more protection from the referees. Bettman was more than willing to listen to the complaints of the goaltenders and the general managers screaming to protect their most prized asset on the ice in most cases. What came out of Bettman's bag of tricks turned a simple idea into an executional nightmare. After a string of goaltender interference incidents leading up to the 1998–99 season, Bettman and the general managers got together and decided to get tough on the goal crease. The new rule stated that if any player was found in the crease when a goal was scored, the goal was automatically called back. It seemed like a solid, rational rule that the referees would have no trouble calling out on the ice. If a player obstructed a goaltender in the crease, thereby stopping him from performing his duties, the goal did not count—simple, right? However, theory doesn't always work in practice.

During the regular season, goal after goal was reviewed, which slowed down the game and angered fans, marketers, coaches and players. But it pleased goaltenders. It was a sad spectacle to watch. Whenever a player came near the goaltender when a goal was scored, the goaltender would immediately look to the ref and point to the crease. The referee was then required to check with the video goal judge to see if any opposing player put so much as a toe in the crease. It was the adult version of the Hot Lava game.

This interference rule caused so many goals to get called back and made players avoid going to the net that goaltenders' goals-against average dropped to record lows during the 1998–99 season, with four netminders having less than 2.00 for the first time since the 1930–31 season. The new rule was widely criticized, and many hoped that Bettman would listen to the growing dissent and change the regulation or at least loosen its application when going into the playoffs. But Bettman stubbornly refused to alter the rule, letting the season take its course. It was just a matter of time before that decision blew up in his face.

After a long playoff, the two teams with the best goaltenders in the league that season, Ed Belfour for the Dallas Stars and Dominic Hasek for the Buffalo Sabres, met in the Stanley Cup finals. Even though both teams had some talented offensive players, the series was noted for its defensive play and rather low-scoring games. The series started out as expected, with a close 3–2 overtime victory by the Sabres. Dallas won the next game by a score of 2–1 to even up the series. The teams then split the next two games before Dallas took game five with a clutch 2–0 shutout of the Sabres.

Buffalo head coach Lindy Ruff was relying on his number one goaltender, Hasek, to help force a game-seven final with a win on home ice, but the Stars came out fast in game six and looked like the team that would win. However, owing to some incredible goaltending by Hasek, the Sabres managed to stay in the game and force an overtime period with the score at two goals apiece. Both teams appeared skittish in the first overtime period, with neither side willing to take an offensive risk to end the game. There were a few more goal-scoring chances in the second overtime period, but again, 20 minutes went by and the teams were still deadlocked.

Into the third overtime period, the players were tired and started taking a few more risks to end the marathon game. Going into the 15th minute of the third overtime, with the puck deep in the Sabres' zone, several Dallas players piled in front of Hasek hoping to snag a loose puck. When the shot came in front of the goal, Hasek managed to get a piece of the puck, but he couldn't smother it, and it fell just off the goal line. Brett Hull quickly caught sight of the puck before anyone else and swatted the disk into the net for the Stanley Cup–winning goal.

While the Dallas bench emptied out onto the ice to celebrate, the Sabres immediately surrounded referee Terry Gregson because Hull's skate had clearly been in the crease at the time he pushed the puck into the net. This had been a routine call during the regular season, but suddenly Gregson made no effort to have the goal reviewed, even though all the fans at home and at the game could see on the instant replay that Hull had indeed put his toe into the hot lava. Head coach Lindy Ruff was livid, hurling nasty words at the referee, who could not hear him over the booing from the partisan Buffalo crowd.

After the dust settled and the Sabres returned to their dressing rooms, the mood was somber. "I'm very bitter because of what happened," said Hasek. "It's a shame."

No one was more upset than Lindy Ruff, who had just lost the Stanley Cup. "I wanted Bettman to answer the question why Hull's goal was not reviewed," spat an angry Ruff. "And really, he just turned his back on me like he knew this might be a tainted goal, and there was no answer for it."

Despite Bettman's arrogant back turn, he must have known that the league got the judgment wrong because just two days after Dallas won the Cup, the league announced that it was dropping the strict interpretation of the in-the-crease rule. But on the night of Dallas' win, to everyone watching the game and to the rest of the sports world, it looked like the league and the referees didn't have the nerve to call back the goal after the celebrations began. Everybody agreed the rule was a dumb one, and that without it, the goal would have been perfectly good, but the Dallas Stars now must live with the historical footnote that their only Stanley Cup win to date was tainted by a toe in the crease.

By the 1999–2000 season, the product on the ice was clearly lacking. The defense-first strategy popularized by the New Jersey Devils was spreading throughout the league. Expansion teams without a hope of winning had embraced the system and were able to succeed. Goal production tumbled, fans began to lose interest in the game and owners started to lose money. From Gretzky's first years in the NHL, when it was common for teams to score 300–350 goals per season, to his retirement in 1999 when top teams were scoring around the 250 goals per season, the NHL was obviously losing its action.

Whether it was the size increase in the goaltenders' equipment or the institution of strange rules, the main factor that led to the slowing down of the fastest team sport in the world was the neutral zone trap system. This system allowed the "less-talented" teams to compete against the top-tier teams in the league. Gary Bettman's expansion brought in more teams, but it also brought in more players, thereby diluting the talent pool and forcing some smaller-market teams to work with what they had. Take, for example, the case of the 1995–96 Florida Panthers.

After witnessing the success the New Jersey Devils had under the neutral zone trap system, the three-year-old expansion franchise Panthers decided after two seasons of mediocre hockey and missing out on the playoffs twice that they would fire head coach Roger Nielson and put in Doug MacLean to implement a new style of playing hockey. The Panthers turned around their fortunes the instant they began to play with the trap. The 1995–96 Panthers were a lot like the 1994–95 New Jersey Devils: low on scoring talent and high on hard-working forwards. The Panthers' games typically ended with scores below three total, but it often turned out in their favor. For the first time since entering the league in 1994, the Florida Panthers had made the playoffs with a winning record of 41–31–10 for 92 points.

They had performed well in the regular season, but few figured the team would go far in the playoffs when up against more prolific scoring teams such as the Pittsburgh Penguins and the Philadelphia Flyers, let alone what the Western Conference put up as competition, among them the powerhouse Detroit Red Wings and the Colorado Avalanche. Although the Panthers' success could be attributed to their system, many fans claimed it was the power of the rat that was pushing the Panthers into the winning column that season.

The story of the rat goes back to the beginning of the season before the opening home game of the 1995–96 regular season. Forward Scott Mellanby was in the team's dressing room, getting ready for the upcoming game, when he saw a rat scurry across the floor. Without hesitating, Mellanby grabbed a stick, curled the rat against the blade and fired the rodent against the wall of the dressing room, killing the vermin instantly. It just so happened that after taking care of the rat, Mellanby went on to score two goals in a Panthers' victory that night.

After the game, Panther goaltender John Vanbiesbrouck told the assembled media about the incident with the rat, saying that Mellanby had accomplished a rare feat in hockey—a "rat trick." Panthers fans seized on the idea, and on occasion during the season, a rubber rat was thrown onto the ice when a player scored. But in the playoffs, the tradition reached new heights. Whenever one of the players scored in a playoff home game, fans responded by tossing out thousands of rats for every goal. Unfortunately for the ice cleaners, but lucky for rubber rat sellers, the deeper into the playoffs the Panthers went, the more rats would hit the ice each game.

The Panthers surprised everyone by completely dominating the Boston Bruins in the opening round. The series saw the Panthers score 12 goals in the first two games as they went on to win the series in five. It was in the Conference semifinals, though, that the Panthers faced their first real opposition in the Philadelphia Flyers and were forced to tighten up on defense and rely on the hot streak goaltending of John Vanbiesbrouck.

The series was tight, hard checking, and like many of their games during the regular season, low scoring, but the Panthers managed to surprise again by beating the Flyers in six games. The power of the rat was strong. After dispatching with the Flyers, the Panthers ran into the power-house Pittsburgh Penguins.

This was a tougher series as the Penguins Jaromir Jagr and captain Mario Lemieux were the more difficult players to catch in the trap system, but again the Panthers prevailed and won in seven games to make it into the finals against the Colorado Avalanche. The power of the rat ran out in the final, though. The Avalanche were too tough to play against. They forced the Panthers out of their trap system and easily defeated the Cinderella team in four straight games.

Despite losing, the Panthers proved the concept of team defense to be effective, and as a result, other teams picked up on it, especially the expansion clubs, and hockey fans were left crying out for some goals.

Chapter Six

Working Through the Growing Pains

Poor Gary Bettman never got to enjoy his hockey honeymoon for long. He did have a few months during his first years when he felt like a real league boss, but his administration had been consistently bombarded by problems from the start. He knew he would be up against some major obstacles.

One of his first issues and tasks as commissioner was to secure the league a broadcasting deal with one of the big American television stations. If the NHL was going to break out of its small-time stature, it needed a shot of American hype to get noticed. It was clear that Bettman needed a television deal, but convincing the networks that the product he was selling was worth buying was a different story.

While Canadians devoured anything hockey, the demographics in the United States showed a widespread apathy toward the game. There was already a sizeable portion of hardcore fans spread out across the States, but in a land of nearly 400 million people on the open sports market, hockey was just a fringe sport. It had equal ranking with beach volleyball and darts in the television standings. If Bettman wanted the game of hockey to hit the big time, he needed to start knocking on the doors of ABC, Fox and NBC to market the game of hockey to as many Americans as possible.

Bettman was keenly aware that the league had to expand in order to survive. However, cities such as Dallas, San Jose and Raleigh did not have a population with prior knowledge of the game, and therefore they would need to be convinced that hockey was a better entertainment option than basketball, baseball or soccer. Thus began his marketing blitz in the U.S. to explain what the game was all about and why people should tune in.

The first push into the U.S. by Bettman started in the marketing department. When Bettman took over the league in 1993, the NHL had no marketing department to speak of. For the old-school owners of the major clubs, the game sold itself. To reach new markets, though, Bettman and his team needed to think big.

When you want to go big, go Hollywood. So the NHL hired a Los Angeles media company to produce a series of commercials that painted the game as a sport where warriors do battle for honor and glory. The TV spots were titled "My NHL," which looked much like a trailer for an Arnold Schwarzenegger or Jet Li action blockbuster.

The setting of one of the commercials starts off in a candlelit room where our hero hockey player sits Zen-like with his shirt off while a woman with a seductive voice narrates a succession of philosophical battle quotations such as, "He wins battles by making no mistakes," and, "He imposes his will on his enemy, but he does not allow his enemy to impose his will on him." A woman then appears from offscreen, wearing virgin-white robes and showing plenty of cleavage. She helps the hockey "warrior" put on his equipment, whispers in his ear, "Ready?" and then he heads for the ice. In a darkened arena, the warrior steps onto the ice in a series of slow-mo, sped-up and altered shots that are designed to add drama and tension to the scene, with a background score that had to be stolen from some epic blockbuster movie.

The commercial was a failure. In Canada, it was met with laughter and derision for the rookie American commissioner who had sanctioned the ad, providing further proof that he was hired to change the fundamentals of the game. The commercial didn't really do much for American audiences, either, other than leaving a few people scratching their heads wondering what the hell they were watching. Was it an ad for a new cologne or an antiperspirant? The league had never tried any such moves before, and Bettman knew he was swimming in uncharted waters, but he had to start somewhere.

With a marketing strategy up and running, Bettman now focused on getting that major TV network deal that hockey needed to enter into the running with the other professional sports. Canada could always be counted on to deliver a few million viewers—and that is just for a single team in one regional viewing area.

The history of hockey broadcasting in the U.S. was spotty at best. Throughout much of the history of the NHL, if Americans wanted to see a hockey game, they had to buy a ticket. There were broadcasts of special games over the years, with NBC and CBS picking up a few games here and there, but no major commitments came from any networks. In 1981, the NHL made its first tentative forays into the American market when it signed a deal with the fledgling USA Network that carried a full schedule of games, under the banner *NHL on USA*.

It was during the USA Network's first season in the hockey world that a younger Don Cherry began his broadcasting career doing the color commentary for a few games. As great as it was to have a regular broadcast of NHL games on American television, the number of viewers tuning in was not high, and to make matters worse, during their first run of the Stanley Cup playoffs in 1981, the network broadcast several regular-season baseball games instead of the important games in hockey. The audience for these hockey games was a decent size but was relatively small compared to what MLB and the NFL were getting on the major networks.

The *NHL on USA* lasted until 1985, when the rights were taken over by ESPN. When the ESPN contract came up in 1988, the NHL then jumped over to the specialty cable station SportsChannel. But that deal was bad for all parties involved. The league was reaching just 15 million households with SportsChannel, and the network itself was losing millions every year. After that contract expired in 1992, interim NHL president Gil Stein signed a new agreement with ESPN for five years; it was worth $125 million for 25 games, some playoffs and all of the finals. At that time, ESPN was owned by the Walt Disney Company, the same parent company of ABC Network, which decided to air a few games on its broadcast

Wide World of Sports. This had a big impact on the league as the network was now reaching 91 percent of American homes, but it was just a small drop in the bucket as ABC only took on a few games.

Gary Bettman knew what the stakes were when he took over as NHL president. "Our not being on television for so long has caused a learning deficit," he once told *New York Magazine.*

The prospects for getting into the television market was not promising. All the other major networks had experimented with broadcasting hockey on their stations but had meager returns. Bettman knew he had a large task ahead of him. But then, like an angel descending from the heavens, Rupert Murdoch arrived on the network television scene.

The Australian media mogul was looking to quickly establish his brand in the hearts and minds of American audiences, and he knew that the best way to do so was through sports. He started in the Fox station in 1987 but didn't achieve notoriety until December 1993, when he paid $1.6 billion for four years of Sunday NFL football and the Super Bowl. It was a major coup for Fox as NFL football had been on CBS for 38 straight years. Seeing the void in CBS' weekend lineup, Bettman was quick to pounce and was in discussions with the network when Fox came in at the last minute and outbid CBS with a $155 million, five-year contract.

The Fox Network had plans for hockey. Hockey is a crash-and-bang sport that displays incredible skills, all wrapped in an epic drama that unfolds over the course of 60 minutes, on solid ice no less. The network wanted to take that fast-paced, frenetic action and splash it across television screens throughout the United States. Fox wanted to give hockey that special American style of "in your face" sports experience that closely resembled the way monster truck rallies are advertised, with loud explosions, shots of beautiful young women and a scary announcer screaming, "This Sunday! Sunday! Sunday! Come on down to…the arena to see Bone Crusher! Sunday! Sunday! Sunday!"

Fox was supposed to begin their coverage of the NHL at the start of the 1994–95 season, but the lockout forced them to put off their plans for a few months. Once the puck hit the ice again, though, Fox was prepared, with commercial and promos that were made to reach out, grab you by the eyelids and force you to watch (if you were a male between 18 and 35). The network played up hockey as being a battle between the stars of the game, using lines such as, "Gretzky's Great, but can he and his St. Louis Blues stop the Red Wings Russian Fab Five, led by Sergei Fedorov?"

This commentary was backed by fancy graphics and shots of on-ice action taken from wacky angles mixed with bad studio acting by the players, all with a pinch of the '90s extreme attitude.

Once Fox and the NHL got Americans to watch hockey, they faced another challenge. Americans were remarkably uneducated about the game. The solution, according to the network, was to take them to "hockey school." The network asked the stars of the NHL to step up, and they reluctantly agreed to speak on hockey's behalf. As a general rule, hockey players should not be put in front of a camera and told to remember lines.

But Fox thought otherwise and produced some memorable TV spots with players such as Rob Blake and Wayne Gretzky reading scripts like B-movie actors with wooden-like voices. "The crease is an area bordered by a red semi-circle, six feet in front of the net," said Blake into the camera, standing by a net in full gear. Hockey purists called for heads to fall, but Fox just kept trying new and crazier innovations, such as the FoxTrax Puck mentioned in a previous chapter in this book.

Although, to be fair, Fox and Bettman knew that diehard hockey fans would stay no matter how the game was packaged. What the network and Bettman really wanted was a new audience.

With a new market opened up in television, the league began to expand south and add new teams. The new team owners and now the new broadcasters, though, were calling for changes in the game.

In order to be more pleasing to viewers and to increase advertising dollars, Fox and several of the new owners lobbied the league to make a few alterations to the game. Had these modifications been implemented, Bettman would have woken up one morning to find a severed moose head in bed with him. (That's how Canadians inform you that a price has been put on your head.) One of the ideas was to move from three periods to two halves of 30 minutes each to help accommodate longer television timeouts. Michael Eisner, head of Disney and owner of the expansion Anaheim Mighty Ducks, wanted a whole slew of changes to help him sell the game, such as using bigger nets to allow more scoring and therefore more action; forcing players to remove their helmets when sitting on the bench so the cameras could get a better look at their faces; and putting a ban on fighting. Disney was, after all, a family-orientated company.

Despite all the flashy graphics and snappy camera angles, not enough Americans were tuning in to watch hockey to make the game profitable.

Although the regular-season ratings were not expected to be high, all hope was pinned on bringing in a record number of viewers during the playoffs, with a last push in the Stanley Cup finals. Fox wanted the Stanley Cup finals to be the new Super Bowl of hockey, but instead, during the network's tenure as NHL broadcasters, it got four consecutive finals series that were swept in four games straight, as well as the controversial 1999 Stanley Cup between the Dallas Stars and the Buffalo Sabres and the FoxTrax debacle.

Despite the game's lackluster beginning on American television, Fox wanted to continue its relationship with hockey and signed a new contract with the league at the end of the 1999 playoffs. That is when Michael Eisner and Disney stepped in and made a better offer to run hockey on its television properties, ABC and ESPN. For the broadcast rights, Disney paid $600 million for a five-year contract period, which was a lot more money than what Fox had paid in 1995.

It soon became apparent that Disney did not want NHL hockey on its main network. In the first year, ABC only aired four games—all on Saturday afternoons. This schedule continued into the playoffs as well, when the American broadcasting giant imposed its will upon Canadian viewers who hated the idea of afternoon playoff games. The folks at CBC tried to get Bettman to hear their complaints, but they fell on deaf ears. Where at least Fox had tried to sell the sport to its American audience, Disney really didn't care all that much, and as a result, ratings dropped significantly.

Bettman could hardly wait until the contract expired in the spring of 2004 to find a new network to take on hockey. But the damage had already been done. Hockey was at its lowest point since Bettman had taken over as NHL boss. Not enough American viewers were jumping on board the hockey brand in order for the league's smaller southern franchises to survive. The league needed butts in the seats at games and at home, and they were not getting that during the late 1990s and into the early millennium. The NHL was losing television revenue, and the game was suffering on the ice as well.

Bettman had been hired to secure the league's economic footing, and it appeared to be wavering once again. He would continually remind people of this fact when the players' collective bargaining agreement came up for renewal in September 2004. The league was on shaky ground, and it needed to shore up a lucrative television deal to get the sport stable once again.

With Fox and CBS out of the picture because of previous deals gone awry, Bettman was left to the only other alternative in the major American market, and that was NBC. He went to them with big dreams and even bigger hopes, but the NBC executives only saw an upward climb in trying to sell the game. Hockey needed a lot of attention in order to survive in the American market, and that attention would cost money.

After the lockout, and with the game hopefully back on financial track, ESPN dropped out of the running for the U.S. cable rights after lowballing Bettman on a new contract. Facing the prospect of not having hockey in American homes, Bettman turned to Comcast and its channel the Outdoor Life Network (OLN).

The OLN was more of a specialty fringe sports channel that showed a lot of fishing shows, was the American home of the Tour de France and broadcast the occasional rodeo. The company was looking to expand its sports presence, however, so it paid well enough for the hockey rights. It was a deal, but it wasn't what Bettman wanted. OLN, which became known as Versus, then the NBC Sports Network, was a small player in the network world.

Even though the NHL now had Sidney Crosby and Alexander Ovechkin as its major stars—who were marketed like crazy—hockey occupies only a small portion of the American sports market. The Super Bowl alone pulled in a record 111 million viewers in 2012, whereas the 2011 Stanley Cup finals between the Boston Bruins and the Vancouver Canucks managed just 8.5 million in the U.S. In Canada, about the same number of people watched the finals on CBC. A nation with a population of approximately 36 million compared with the 315 million in the U.S. speaks to the wide gap in attention paid toward hockey in the two countries.

Slowly, though, the hype began to build around the NHL as Sidney Crosby and the Penguins provided some excellent hockey drama in the 2007 and 2008 playoffs when the marketers' dream, Sidney Crosby, won his first Stanley Cup. The game was sold as being faster and more exciting, and it was. With a renewed interest in a more economically viable NHL, the television networks were now knocking on Bettman's door.

In 2011, Comcast and its Versus network merged with NBC Universal, and NBC decided to continue its relationship with the NHL, but this time around, the price was much higher. NBC paid a record $2 billion for the broadcast rights to the NHL over the next 10 years. The deal was almost too good to be true. NBC committed to showing

100 regular-season hockey games on its network stations as well as its other cable assets and broadcasting every playoff game. Finally, the NHL could stand up in a crowd and get noticed; that's all Bettman ever wanted. He felt if hockey were given a chance to take root in U.S. soil, Americans would fall in love with the game.

Chapter Seven

Love Him or Hate Him

From about 1995 to 2004, the product the NHL was selling needed a boost. In Canada, hockey's popularity was still growing at a steady pace. It helped that the Calgary Flames and the Edmonton Oilers both made Stanley Cup final runs during that time, but unfortunately, neither of the Canadian teams won a championship, losing to the Tampa Bay Lightning and the Carolina Hurricanes, respectively.

Always looking for new ways to sell the game, Gary Bettman decided to take professional NHL hockey back to its roots—outdoors. He had eagerly watched the National Collegiate Athletic Association (NCAA) experiment in the 2001 outdoor hockey game between the University of Michigan and Michigan State University.

The game took place at Spartan Stadium in East Lansing, Michigan, before a record crowd of

74,544 sitting out in the freezing cold to watch two university teams battle it out. If it worked for a university game, thought Bettman, then why wouldn't it work for the best hockey players in the world? People would surely turn out to see that.

The NHL played around with the idea of an outdoor game and came up with the Heritage Classic. The event would mirror the American college game in that it would be played outdoors in front of a large, freezing-cold audience. Obviously, playing the game in Tampa Bay or Dallas was out of the question, so the NHL decided to host the game in the coldest city they could think of—Edmonton. The teams involved were the Montreal Canadiens and, of course, the Edmonton Oilers.

When the game was announced, Gary Bettman earned some street credibility with the hockey purists of the world, who had started foaming at the mouth when the idea was just a rumor. Not only would the NHL put on a regular-season game outdoors, but they would also bring out some of the old-time legends from both teams to play a short exhibition game prior to the Canadiens–Oilers "real" game. For the icing on the cake, Wayne Gretzky agreed to put his skates back on for the first time since retiring in 1999 to play in the old-timers game with some of his former linemates such as Mark Messier (who was still playing in the NHL at the time and received special permission to attend), goaltender Grant Fuhr and Paul Coffey. They would play against a team of Canadiens alumni that included Guy Lafleur, Steve Shutt and Larry Robinson.

Hockey fans across Canada completely bought in to the event, and people were planning hockey pilgrimages to Edmonton in the hopes of being one of the people lucky enough to get a seat (though "lucky" is a relative term, considering the temperature fell to −30°C [−22°F] with the wind chill).

The first Heritage Classic was played on November 22, 2003, before a shivering crowd of 57,167 at Edmonton's Commonwealth Stadium, normally the home of the Edmonton Eskimos of the CFL. Being Canadian, most fans were used to the freezing temperatures, but they came prepared, with plenty of layers of clothing, toe warmers and a few pre-game shots of whiskey. Fans showed up, some even an hour and a half before the start of the event, from all across Canada. The game had struck a chord in the hearts of passionate hockey fans. Canadian hockey fans tend to wax poetic when caught up in the remembrance of all things hockey and about the good ole days of the game, whether professionally or personally. It brought back memories of playing the game because you loved it so much that you were willing to play outside in frigid conditions for hours on end. The Heritage Classic represented what hockey meant to so many Canadians, and even the players themselves got wrapped up in the whole excitement of the event. Gary Bettman had scored the game-winning marketing goal.

By the time the game was ready to start, the thousands in attendance were primed to watch some classic hockey. The old-timers game was probably the most anticipated match of the night, considering that Gretzky was making his return to hockey in an Edmonton uniform for the first time since that sad day in August 1988 when he was traded to the Los Angeles Kings. During the introduction of the old-timers lineup, the crowd applauded for the hockey greats Guy Lafleur, Charlie Huddy, Larry Robinson, Marty McSorley, Jari Kurri and Dave Semenko, but when Wayne Gretzky's name was announced, the temperature rose a few degrees with the warmest applause of night for the Great One, wearing his familiar Oilers number 99 jersey.

The retired Canadiens and the old-time Oilers were to play two 15-minute periods of hockey, and most people expected an easy-flowing game with plenty of camaraderie between former opponents, but the players stepped up and put on an impressive performance. Grant Fuhr provided one of the highlights of the game when he made one of his signature glove saves on a Stephane Richer snap shot that was destined for the top corner. Another highlight was seeing Gretzky in his office behind the Montreal net trying to set up a goal. At the end of the two periods, though, it was the unlikely "fourth line" trio of Ken Linseman, Marty McSorley and Dave Semenko that made the difference in the game, with goals by Linseman and McSorley. Grant Fuhr and Bill Ranford got the shutout.

"Listen, we are not as good as we used to be, not a chance," Gretzky told NHL.com at the time. "But, we had a lot of fun out there. Both teams gave a lot of effort, and the fans were tremendous. It was a great day for hockey."

Team management then echoed that sentiment.

"It seemed everybody in Canada needed to be there that weekend," said Patrick LaForge, the Edmonton Oilers president. "It was magical."

After the veterans left the ice, the actual regular-season game between the Oilers and the Canadiens started. Apart from the players being outdoors and wearing a few extra layers, the game was just like any other NHL game. The only major difference was that goaltender Jose Theodore played the entire game with a Canadiens toque fixed over top his helmet.

"I remember that my mom always said, 'Put a toque on—you're going to catch a cold,'" Theodore said after the game. "So I decided to make sure she's not going to say anything when I go back home, so I put a toque on." The red Habs toques became an instant hit with hockey fans and became a bestseller.

For the game itself, the Canadiens Richard Zednik opened the scoring in the second period and also netted the goal for the 4–3 winner for Montreal. At the end of the game, fans shuffled out of the stadium in search of a place to warm their tushies and talk about what they had just seen. Losing head coach Craig MacTavish put the game into perspective: "It was a great day with one exception. They got the better of the bounces."

The outdoor experience was a complete success because everyone left happy. The fans loved seeing the old timers, highlighted of course by Gretzky and the nostalgia of watching an outdoor game. The players enjoyed being a part of something new and unique. Bettman was overjoyed at the success of the game because the advertisers loved it, and hockey was portrayed in a positive light. A measure of the event's success was seen in the moment the game was over—everyone was knocking on Bettman's door asking when the next one would be held.

Plans for another game began immediately. The 2004–05 lockout postponed the next outdoor game, but Bettman was not going to let this marketing gold mine just disappear. It took a while to find the right teams and the right venue, but the league finally announced that the first Winter Classic was to be played between the Pittsburgh Penguins and the Buffalo Sabres in Orchard Park, New York, on January 1, 2008. A crowd of 71,217 people gathered to watch the game at Ralph Wilson Stadium. Luckily for these fans, the temperature at game time hovered just above the freezing mark, making for a pleasant viewing experience compared to the Edmonton Heritage Classic. Pittsburgh won the game 2–1 in a shootout on a goal from Penguins captain Sidney Crosby.

The event went off without a hitch and proved popular among the American hockey fans. As a result, the NHL has scheduled a Winter Classic every year since 2008. Although a complete success on all levels, the outdoor games did not make all fans happy. The Winter Classic was hyped as the event of the year for hockey in North America, but Canadian hockey fans were feeling left out of the loop, as no Canadian team had played in the marquee event. Sure, the league had put on the 2003 and 2011 Heritage Classics, both with Canadian franchises (Habs twice—once versus the Oilers and then the Flames). But Canadian teams had the sneaking suspicion that the Heritage Classic was just an afterthought for the league, an appeasement by Bettman. They were right to be suspicious. While the league was more than happy to give the Winter Classic twice to the Penguins and Philadelphia Flyers, Canadian clubs were left scratching their heads. The NHL even said no to the Montreal Canadiens during the 2008–09 season when an outdoor game was proposed to help celebrate the team's 100th anniversary.

George Johnson of the *Calgary Herald* told NHL commissioner Gary Bettman about the feeling in Canada about the outdoor games, telling Bettman in a February 2011 interview, "In some quarters, the Heritage Classic is being portrayed as nothing more or less than an appeasement to cranky Canadians—as the underprivileged child hidden underneath the stairs in comparison to the New Year's Day Winter Classic."

Bettman's response was sharp. "That's absurd. It's baseless," he said. "It's someone looking for something on a slow news day, looking for something to write or say, to be critical for no reason."

However, it was hard to argue with the facts. The Winter Classic had received the league's full promotional support, with ads, commercials and even the HBO 24/7 show that gave a behind-the-scene's look, documentary style, into the event. In comparison, the 2011 Heritage Classic between the Montreal Canadiens and the Calgary Flames barely made news outside Canada. (The Canadiens lost by a score of 4–0.)

Bettman put an end to Canadians' whining when he announced that the Toronto Maple Leafs would face off against the Detroit Red Wings at the Winter Classic in January 2013. That event, however, was postponed to the 2013–14 season because of the lockout.

It seemed that for every success Bettman has achieved in his tenure as NHL head honcho, there have been a litany of problems that have passed across his desk. A constant source of headache for him since he entered the league has been the issue of the violence of the game. Barely a few months into his job in 1993, he handed out the most severe punishment in league history when he suspended Dale Hunter for a dirty hit on Pierre Turgeon. Bettman had hoped to set the tone in his administration's response to violent offenders in the game and avoid further incidents in the future.

However, unlike other sports, as Bettman would quickly learn, hockey is a different animal. When you have large men playing one of the fastest team sports in the world, on a hard ice surface, armed with sticks and with sharp blades attached to their feet and who are all competing for the same thing, there is bound to be the occasional incident or dustup. Incidents kept creeping up in the game, and reporters kept asking Bettman what he was going to do about all the violence, especially since he wanted to sell the game to American families.

The problem of violence in hockey has always been a controversial topic. Some of the earliest newspaper reports from around the late 1800s about the emerging sport tell of brutal fights between players, between players and officials, and between players and fans. There was even a report of a fight between hockey players and figure skaters (they were a lot tougher in those days) who fought over ice time. Most people who look back to the sport around the 1900s imagine gentlemen with well-manicured hair and waxed mustaches playing a civilized game. The reality of the game back then, though, is far different.

In one of those games from the supposed gentlemanly era, the sport of hockey faced its first major scandal. On March 8, 1907, the Cornwall

Hockey Club and the Ottawa Victorias faced off for a game in the four-team Federal Amateur Hockey League (FAHL). Being a four-team league, both teams were well acquainted with each other and had built up bad blood before the start of this particular game.

The game was quiet for the first half (games back then had two 30 minute halves), but by the second half, several players from both sides began to take liberties on the ice and tension quickly mounted. Cornwall forward Owen McCourt was the most physical of the players, and his main target that night was Ottawa's Arthur Throop. But it was Throop that got the better of McCourt, taking him hard into the boards. McCourt, however, would get his revenge. After shaking off the hit, he skated directly at Throop with his stick raised above his shoulders, then swung his stick down like an ax, hitting Throop above the eye. It opened up a huge gash that sent a gush of blood across the ice. As players began to square off in a post-whistle rumble, Ottawa's Charles Masson struck back, cracking his stick over McCourt's head in revenge.

McCourt fell to the ice, and when the melee died down, he was taken to the dressing room. He returned to the Cornwall bench several minutes later, then was taken to the hospital after complaining of dizziness and a headache. Hours later, McCourt died in hospital. Local officials wasted little time in the wake of his death, promptly arresting Masson and charging him with one count of murder.

In court, Cornwall captain Reddy McMillan testified that Masson had skated in from about 40 feet away while McCourt was fighting another Ottawa player, but other witnesses testified that McCourt may have been hit by another player before Masson struck him. This was enough for the judge, who believed that Masson "may have acted in self-defense." The charge was downgraded from murder to manslaughter. When the judge returned his verdict, Charles Masson was absolved of the murder in a finding of "not guilty." The judge ruled that the conflicting evidence did not sufficiently prove that Masson's attack had been the fatal blow.

Since the creation of the National Hockey League in 1917, there has been an ongoing debate about the role of violence and fighting in the game. The stance on fighting was firm. When a fight happened, both players were ejected from the game. In 1918, however, the league introduced the two blue lines, and with that came the advent of forward passing, though only in the neutral zone. The introduction of the lines changed the nature of the game. Where there was once open ice, now the attacking team had less real estate in which to maneuver. This led to more collisions and more fights.

The NHL had the power back then to stop the fighting by taking a firm stand, but in 1922, the league chose to keep it as part of the game. That year, Rule 56 was enacted, which regulated fighting and gave the offending players a five-minute penalty rather than an ejection. Fighting, after all, was proving popular with the fans, and the league did not want to lose them. Not only was fighting tolerated by the league in those early days, but it was also used heavily in promoting hockey when the league first expanded into the United States.

No one was better at promoting fighting than New York Rangers founder Tex Rickard. After noticing sluggish ticket sales during the team's first season in 1926–27, Rickard, an experienced boxing promoter, knew which aspects of the game to focus on in order to get fans into seats. Before a game, Rickard hired ambulances to blare their sirens through the streets of Manhattan on their way toward Madison Square Garden, luring out the curious to see what all the commotion was about. When the Boston Bruins came to town, Rickard played a masterstroke of marketing and plastered the city with "Wanted: Dead or Alive" posters of the Bruins' most hated and violent villain, Eddie Shore. The marketing worked, and fans showed up in droves just to boo the "evil" Eddie Shore.

Let's face the facts. Many hockey fans love the violence. Watch any game when two players drop their gloves, and every fan in the arena will immediately stand up and cheer wildly for their favorite player to take the head off the other guy. As recently as the 2012 Stanley Cup playoffs, network viewing numbers indicated that the more contentious and violent the games, the more people will watch. For example, the Pittsburgh Penguins–Philadelphia Flyers series in 2012 was rife with bad blood, violence and the occasional fight, and that series gave both the American and Canadian broadcasters some of their highest ratings of the playoffs.

Bettman is aware of this aspect of hockey and has consistently treaded carefully on the subject when a major incident of violence occurs in the game. At a 2007 press conference, he gave a cautious response when asked about fighting in hockey: "Fighting has always had a role in the game...from a player safety standpoint, what happens in fighting is something we need to look at just as we need to look at hits to the head. But we're not looking to have a debate on whether fighting is good or bad or should be part of the game."

As commissioner, Bettman knows better than anyone that if the physical edge were removed from the game, he would face a shrinking audience, upset advertisers and an angry cadre of team owners. Even Bettman's former colleague, the man who once had the responsibility as the NHL chief disciplinarian, Colin Campbell (1998–2011) said in Adam Proteau's excellent book, *Fighting the Good Fight: Why On-Ice Violence Is Killing Hockey,* "We sell hate. Our game sells hate."

The subject of violence in the game is one that Canada's grumpy old man Don Cherry loves to talk about during his brief airtime on CBC's *Hockey Night in Canada:* "The people who yell and scream about hockey violence are a handful of intellectuals and newspapermen who never pay to get in to see a game. The fans, who shell out the money, have always like good, rough hockey."

As much as hockey fans seemed to enjoy the violence, a few incidents received global media attention and forced those who watch or sell the game to wonder if all the violence was worth the cost. Fortunately for Bettman, he has never had to deal with a case of murder on the ice, but these more-violent incidents proved that the extreme might not be far off.

Marty McSorley made his hockey career as a fighter and lived strictly by the fighters' code of conduct, that unwritten, often confusing set of made-up rules by which fighting is supposed to govern itself in all of hockey. He took pride in his role and played it perfectly, making a name for himself as Wayne Gretzky's protector through much of the Great One's career. But McSorley's career of incredible highs ended on an incredible low during a game in Vancouver in 2000.

On February 21, 2000, McSorley, then with the Boston Bruins, rolled into Vancouver for a battle against the Canucks. The game promised to be a tense one since McSorley and the Canucks heavyweight enforcer Donald Brashear had previously done battle with each other during the season, and they had some unfinished business. During the first shift of the game, the two tough guys met on the ice to settle their score. In the fight, Brashear got the better of the veteran fighter before tackling him to the ice. But as the linesmen were separating the two, Brashear took the opportunity to give McSorley one last shot to the face while he was down. Brashear then made the situation worse by taunting McSorley in the penalty box, dusting off his hands as if to say, "I win." Under the fighter's code, this insult required another battle, and once back out on the ice, McSorley did everything he could to get Brashear to drop his gloves, but the Canucks fighter would not oblige.

Angry at the obvious sign of disrespect, on their next shift together out on the ice, McSorley skated over to Brashear and delivered a vicious cross-check to Brashear's kidneys for which McSorley was handed a 10-minute misconduct. As McSorley sat in the sin bin, Brashear took a few more liberties out on the ice while in front of Bruins goaltender Byron Dafoe. In the heat of the action, Brashear ended up falling on Dafoe and took the Bruins' netminder out of the game and the rest of the season. McSorley fumed in the penalty box and planned his attack once he was released. As the code of hockey dictates, "You mess with my goalie, and you're gonna get a fight."

With time winding down in the game, which the Canucks were winning 5–2, McSorley pursued Brashear all over the ice to try to get him to answer for his misdeeds. Brashear ignored him and refused to drop the gloves. With just two seconds left on the clock, McSorley's rage got the better of him, and he swung his stick at Brashear in a final attempt to get him to fight. But instead of slashing him, across the upper arm, McSorley hit Brashear squarely on the temple.

Brashear immediately fell backwards, out cold from the sudden hit, and landed on the hard ice.

His body began to seize. Fans both at the game and watching at home gasped at the sight of Brashear twitching on the ice. Brashear was quickly put on a stretcher and rushed off to hospital, where doctors said he had suffered a grand mal seizure and a severe concussion.

Brashear ended up missing 20 games, but for McSorley, the incident marked the end of his career. The NHL was quick to act and banned him from the league for one year—the longest suspension in league history at the time. But things got worse for the veteran tough guy when a British Columbia provincial court charged him with assault with a weapon and later found him guilty.

Immediately following the verdict, Bettman made a comment:

> *The court today said that its focus was solely on the charge against Mr. McSorley. This was not a trial of the game or the NHL. Clearly, this incident was not representative of NHL hockey or NHL players. While the court's decision today brings closure to this aspect of the incident, it does not alter our position that we will continue to punish severely acts of inappropriate conduct in our game. I believe I owe it both to this player and to all others present and future NHL players to impose a suspension of a definite and ascertainable length. I simply cannot in*

good conscience justify imposing a suspen-
sion of less than one calendar year given the
nature of the incident in question, regardless
of the effect that suspension may have on Mr.
McSorley's career.

For McSorley's crime, the court dealt him an 18-month conditional discharge. He sat out the remainder of the year and decided to retire after the season ended.

Gary Bettman wanted to put the incident out of his mind, but the story went international and brought a focus on hockey that the NHL commissioner did not want. Although the story disappeared from international and American news media within a day or two, the Canadian media would not relent, running feature pieces about the incident on the evening news and long articles in the weekend edition of papers across the Great White North. Concerned parents were wondering whether they should let their kids enroll in local hockey, and people flooded radio call-in shows with plans to boycott the league unless something was done. Basically, everyone was in an uproar.

Bettman tried his best to answer questions and assuage the fears of advertisers that the league was not a violent place and that the McSorley incident was an anomaly in an otherwise peaceful game. A few months later, the playoffs started, and people seemed to forget that a man had nearly died on NHL ice. It was hoped that the incident was just a one-time event that occasionally occurs in professional sports, but the issue of violence in the game would not go away and became the nagging thorn in Gary Bettman's side as other incidents kept creeping up.

On February 16, 2004, the Vancouver Canucks met up to play the Colorado Avalanche in Denver. Both teams were well acquainted with each other but had not built up much of a rivalry. Everything would change that night.

Late in the game, with the Canucks nursing a 1–0 lead, Vancouver captain Markus Naslund led his line up the ice on a rush. As he made his way through the neutral zone, the puck got away from him, and as he stretched out to retrieve it, Colorado forward Steve Moore swerved into him at high speed and struck him hard. Naslund saw the hit coming only at the last second so was unable to avoid the collision. The hit sent him spinning in the air, and he ended up landing face first onto the ice. He was knocked unconscious, but fortunately, his visor protected him from breaking his nose, though he still suffered a concussion, a jagged cut on his forehead and a hyper-extended elbow.

Referees did not call a penalty on the play, and further review by the league disciplinary body agreed that it was a hockey play and an unfortunate incident, but no more than that. Legal or not, the Vancouver Canucks were angry, to say the least. Canucks general manager Brian Burke was livid: "It's obvious the player dropped down to hit him at head level. This was a chance to take out a star player and he took it."

Steve Moore, for his part, claimed innocence, saying that he was just trying to finish his check. But the Canucks were not buying the excuse. The code of letting up when a player is dangerously exposed seemed long removed from the sport, and at the time, concussions to star players were becoming more common. The league had yet to step in to protect the players aside from a few comments from Bettman that they were looking into the matter.

Canucks tough guy Brad May chimed in and wanted to deal with Moore in the old-fashioned hockey way, threatening that there would be a bounty on his head the next time the Canucks played Colorado. Canucks forward Todd Bertuzzi, normally not one for fighting, said that Moore needed to be careful the next time he was out on the ice. Luckily for the Canucks, Naslund's injuries were not as severe as first thought, and he missed only three games. Coincidentally, Naslund's first game back just happened to be against the Colorado Avalanche.

Because of all the inflammatory language prior to the game, Gary Bettman, along with his head disciplinarian Colin Campbell, attended the March 3 game to make sure the players behaved like gentlemen. The game passed without much of a fuss, ending in a 5–5 tie. There were two fights, one between Avs enforcer Peter Worrell and Canucks tough guy Wade Brookbank and the other a minor tussle between Todd Bertuzzi and Avs defenseman Adam Foote, but nothing that the league would have to sanction. Steve Moore remained untouched the entire game.

With the game over and the settling of accounts done between the teams' two enforcers, there was hope that the drama had ended, but hockey players have long memories, and a few days later, they were back at it. The March 9 game was expected to end without incident since the two teams had "settled" their scores, but the Canucks wanted more. The atmosphere in the arena grew more tense in the first period when the Avalanche jumped to a 5–0 lead. Moore dropped the gloves in between the goals to fight Canucks pest Matt Cooke. The fight did not last more than a few seconds, but Moore felt he had answered the call of the code. The Canucks, though, were still out for revenge and spent most of their shifts on the ice harassing him and trying to get him to fight.

In the third period, with almost eight minutes left in a blowout game, Moore was again challenged by minor-league call-up tough guy Sean Pronger, but Moore wanted nothing to do with the rookie and simply skated away. Seeing him back out of another fight incensed Canucks forward Todd Bertuzzi who skated behind Moore and began tugging at his jersey, trying to goad him into a fight. When the hulking forward's invitation was declined, Bertuzzi, still with his gloves on, sucker punched Moore right on the temple. The Avs forward was knocked out cold and fell face first onto the ice, followed by all of Bertuzzi's 240 pounds landing on his back.

As the rest of the players piled in and chose their dancing partners, everyone suddenly paused when they saw that Moore was not moving. Even the crowd that had been calling for blood seconds earlier was now silent as trainers worked on Moore. In an all-too-familiar scene in the NHL in those days, the team trainers immobilized Moore and rushed him to hospital. Moore suffered a severe concussion and three fractured vertebrae in his neck. He was lucky to still have use of his legs. In the Canucks' dressing room after the game, the players expressed their sympathies toward Moore and said that they never wanted to see anything like that happen to anyone.

The next day, Bertuzzi faced the press and had to fight back tears in his public apology to Moore. "Steve, I just want to apologize for what happened out there and that I feel awful for what transpired," he said, fighting back his emotions. "To the fans of hockey, and the fans of Vancouver, for the kids that watch this game, I'm truly sorry. I don't play the game that way. I'm not a mean-spirited person. I'm sorry for what happened."

To the credit of Bettman and the league, they acted quickly in suspending Todd Bertuzzi for the rest of the season and the playoffs. The Vancouver Police Department also investigated and, months later, charged Bertuzzi with assault causing bodily harm. He pleaded guilty to the charge, receiving a conditional discharge with 20 hours of community service. It also cost Bertuzzi heavily. He lost about $500,000 in salary and about $350,000 in lost endorsement deals because advertisers did not want to be associated with Bertuzzi's image.

As for the 26-year-old Steve Moore, the prognosis was much worse. He would never play hockey again. The news was devastating, but he wasn't willing to let the issue get swept under the rug. Still suffering concussion symptoms years later, Moore filed a civil lawsuit in the province of

Ontario in February 2006 against Bertuzzi, the Canucks and the parent company of the Canucks, Orca Bay Sports and Entertainment. Commissioner Bettman did not like all the bad press in the media and tried to get Moore and all other parties to settle out of court, doing his best to mediate the process but to no avail. After several delays, in April 2013 the case of Moore versus Bertuzzi and Co. was brought before a judge and is still underway at the time of this writing.

Moore just wanted to see changes in the league and how it dealt with the culture of violence in the game. "The attack has been bad for our game," he said in a CBC interview. "I don't want to be the cause for any more negativity to the NHL. My biggest hope is that there's a serious evaluation of preventing this from happening again. There's been so much damage to the game. When you talk to people who don't know the game, the only thing you hear is that it's so violent."

The violence issue was one that Gary Bettman had been dealing with his entire career as NHL commissioner. His first experience was in handing out a 21-game suspension to Dale Hunter for his hit on Pierre Turgeon, and then came the Bertuzzi incident. In most cases, Bettman and his support team have done a good job at punishing the bad guys of the game; however, they also know that violence is part of what sells the game to millions around the world. NHL hockey is not like European hockey, nor is it like hockey at a major tournament. It is a rough and physical game, in both body and heart, and is not meant for the weak. But the line is clearly drawn in cases like Bertuzzi and McSorley, where an altercation is viewed as revenge-based, and the league will come down hard.

As if injuries on the ice as the result of violence weren't enough to contend with, Bettman was also having to deal with a rash of injuries to players caused by hits to the head. It was almost becoming epidemic at times. Several players had already had their careers stopped short because of concussions, most notably Keith Primeau, Eric Lindros and Pat LaFontaine.

Although concussions had always been an issue in hockey, in the old days, players were expected to shake off injuries and get back out on the ice. It wasn't considered "manly" to complain, as most coaches would not allow their players to sit out because of "a little headache." However, as time went on, and the league learned more about the seriousness of hits to the head, it tried to protect the players by instituting rules and regulations where head shots were concerned, but the injuries were adding up.

The hit that Scott Stevens delivered to Paul Kariya in the 2003 Stanley Cup finals left the small Ducks forward unconscious on the ice for several long seconds until he suddenly came to, gasping for breath. With Kariya's history of concussions, the hit by Stevens probably shortened his career by a few years. The issue with this incident, as with the Steve Moore hit on Markus Naslund, was that it targeted a player in a vulnerable position with his head hanging low. Scott Stevens might have delivered a textbook check, but he came in on Kariya's blind spot and connected his shoulder with his opponent's head. The league deemed the hit to be a normal everyday hockey play, saying that Kariya had just been unfortunate enough to run into the brick wall that was Stevens.

Other examples of head injuries were piling up, and they were getting more and more vicious, with Bettman refusing to tackle the position straight on:

• February 1994: The Los Angeles Kings Tony Granato's overhead two-handed swing of his stick to the head of Chicago Blackhawks Neil Wilkinson left the Hawks player passed out cold on the ice. Granato got a 15-game suspension.

• February 2001: San Jose Sharks forward Owen Nolan received an 11-game suspension for his hit to the head of the Dallas Stars' Grant Marshall.

• May 2001: Toronto Maple Leafs tough guy Tie Domi delivered a vicious elbow to the head of New Jersey Devils Scott Niedermayer during the 2001 playoff Conference semifinal series. Domi was suspended for 11 games.

• April 2012: The Phoenix Coyotes Raffi Torres got a 25-game suspension for delivering a vicious hit to the head of Chicago Blackhawks star Marian Hossa.

Although the league suspended the offending players (some deserving way more time away from the game than they received), there have been many more cases where Bettman and his crew have fallen short of taking a stance on the headhunters of the NHL, even with the mounting evidence.

In October 2009, the Florida Panthers David Booth is taken off the ice on a stretcher after Philadelphia Flyers forward Mike Richards purposely targeted Booth's head, sending the Panthers forward flying into the air and slamming into the ice face first. "I do believe the league will act appropriately," said Randy Sexton, general manager of the Panthers. "There's been a lot of discussion about taking out those type of hits, especially to the head. I have full confidence that after the league has a chance to review it, they'll take appropriate action."

Flyers general manager Paul Holmgren disagreed. "I don't expect anything," Holmgren said of supplementary discipline. "It was a good hit. Mike's doing his job, he's backtracking. He went to finish his check on a player. His feet never left the ice. I feel bad for Booth, hopefully he's going to be all right. But there was nothing dirty about that hit." Although Mike Richards was assessed a five-minute major for interference and a game misconduct, the league disciplinarian called the incident unfortunate and deemed it a hockey play.

In March 2010, in a game against the Boston Bruins, Pittsburgh Penguins forward Matt Cooke does almost the exact same thing as Mike Richards and knocks out Bruins forward Marc Savard. The hit was so severe that Savard never really recovered from the concussion and was forced into early retirement. In the replay of the video, you can clearly see Cooke target Savard's head, yet he did not receive a penalty or a suspension from the league. This was made all the more insulting because Cooke was known for delivering cheap shots and had a long history that suggested he was the type of the player who would do this on purpose. Even his fellow teammate Bill Guerin had trouble defending Cooke's actions. "If a guy gets hurt like that with a shot to the head, there's got to be something," said Guerin, adding that he expected Cooke to be suspended. "I understand he [Cooke] is on my team but, hey, he's in a tough spot."

Even though the league did not act when it should have and suspend Cooke, Bettman did step up afterward with a proposal. He immediately entered into the rulebook a prohibition against blindside hits to the head. In announcing the rule, Bettman said, "The elimination of these types of hits should significantly reduce the number of injuries, including concussions, without adversely affecting the level of physicality in the game." Some found it odd that the NHL had said there was no problem with the hit but at the same time issued a decree banning malicious headhunting. It seemed to be part of the delicate balance Bettman has always played when it came to violence in the game.

In March 2011, it was a typical Boston Bruins versus Montreal Canadiens game. Emotions were high, the crowd was abuzz and the players were skating hard and hitting even harder. The tone of the game turned more contentious as the Canadiens were leading 4–0 by the second period. With over 23 seconds on the clock, the play began in the Canadiens' zone, and after a faceoff, the puck was shot out into the neutral zone. Canadiens forward Max Pacioretty darted for the puck but was being closely monitored by

6-foot-9, 250-pound Bruins giant defenseman Zdeno Chara. If Chara missed his coverage, Pacioretty would have a clear lane toward the Bruins' net. Pacioretty tried to squeeze past Chara along the boards, but Chara caught up to him and gave him an extra shove, directing Pacioretty's head directly into the glass partition between the players' benches. The sound of his head ringing against the boards could be heard over the noise of the building, known to be the loudest in the NHL. Pacioretty slumped to the ice.

The sight of Pacioretty's body lying motionless on the ice instantly hushed the Montreal crowd. In what felt like hours, not seconds, fans at the game, at home and the players on the ice watched and waited for Pacioretty to move. No Canadiens players could come close to matching the size or strength of Chara, so there was no immediate retribution, but then Canadiens forward Scott Gomez skated over to Chara and seemed to ask him why he would do such a thing.

Meanwhile, the paramedics had secured Pacioretty's head and then put him onto a stretcher to be whisked off to the hospital. Pacioretty was diagnosed with a severe concussion and a nondisplaced fracture in his neck. If he had been hit a little harder or at a different angle, the outcome could have been much worse for both Pacioretty and Chara.

Zdeno Chara's hit seemed like a clear-cut intent in injure to all those that had witnessed the play. Pacioretty and Chara had a history that season of getting on each other's nerves, and Chara had made it clear that they were not best friends. Despite the evidence and the league's past attempts at taking a firm stance against punishing shots to the head, the NHL failed to act once again. The league said that it had trouble divining Chara's intent on the play and again called it an unfortunate hockey play.

Gary Bettman, who was seen as a permanent enemy in the eyes of all Habs fans, young and old, commented on the Chara hit, saying, "It was a horrific injury, we're sorry that it happened in our fast-paced physical game, but I don't think whether or not supplemental discipline was imposed would change what happened." For Bettman, that ended the affair, but the rabid Habs fans were not going to let the incident get swept aside. Phone calls flooded the sports radio talk shows with fans of the Habs and hockey in general crying foul that Chara wasn't penalized. One radio host went as far as asking his listeners to call 911 and report that a crime had been committed on the ice at the Bell Centre. The 911 call centre received so many calls that its computers nearly crashed. Newspaper headlines were no less bombastic in their contempt of the NHL and its figurehead Gary

Bettman. If the league was not going to do something, Quebec's provincial director of criminal prosecutions was going to ask the Montreal police to investigate. It looked as if the NHL might have another Marty McSorley incident on its hands. None of this seemed to faze Bettman, who continued to repeat that the matter had been dealt with and that no further comments would be made.

However, Bettman's ears quickly perked up when Calvin Rovinescu, CEO of Air Canada (the official airline sponsor of the NHL) and an ardent hockey fan, saw the incident and was disgusted enough to write a strongly worded letter to Bettman and the presidents of all the league's franchises. He wrote, "While we support countless sports, arts and community events, we are having difficulty rationalizing our sponsorship of hockey. Unless the NHL takes immediate actions with serious suspensions to the players in question to curtail these life-threatening injuries, Air Canada will withdraw its sponsorship."

Bettman scoffed at the letter, perhaps saying a few choice words in private about the Air Canada CEO, and then flashed his trademark smirk in front of the television cameras and basically told Rovinescu he was free to leave. Bettman had called the airline's bluff and dared Air Canada and several other sponsors to back out on the millions of business dollars they all raked in. "Air Canada is a great brand, as is the National Hockey League, and if they decide that they need to do other things with their sponsorship dollars, that's their prerogative," Bettman told reporters in Washington following a meeting on Capitol Hill. "Just like it's the prerogative of our clubs that fly on Air Canada to make other arrangements if they don't think Air Canada is giving them the appropriate level of service."

The NHL's business partners once again stood down. Gary Bettman was the king of the castle in that moment. He was guarding the interests of the league like a pit bull—it might not be the friendliest of dogs, but it gets the job done. Bettman had chosen his stance on the Pacioretty issue and was not going to be persuaded otherwise. The commissioner would not even move on special directives from several club owners to take immediate action. A flurry of phone calls ensued between Bettman and the rank-breaking owners. The employees bit the hand of their owner, and the owner backed down somewhat.

During offseason meetings with owners and general managers, Bettman agreed to a few changes, including the installation of extra padding on all glass partitions in the arenas league wide and the implementation of heavy fines for players and coaches involved in an incident. The concessions weren't much, but when word of Pacioretty's amazing recovery went public, the situation fell out of the major news cycle, and as he always does, Bettman moved forward and so did hockey.

Gary Bettman can never be accused of conducting business as usual. In his tenure as NHL boss, he has tried things that have completely failed, such as the FoxTrax Puck and the toe-in-the-crease rule, while his other ideas were a success, such as the Winter Classic. But his failures far outshine his well-earned successes.

On the issue of violence and protecting the players, it can be said that he has moved too slowly, but he has walked that fine line between attracting attention to the game because of the physical violence and the players' athletic finesse. Through it all, he has always maintained that his decisions were based on making the game better.

Chapter Eight

End of a Season

Work on the new collective bargaining agreement between the NHL and the NHL Players' Association that was set to expire in September 2004 began in early January 2003. Gary Bettman had hoped to nip the impending problem in the bud by having a series of frank discussions with all parties involved. His motivation often came down to numbers, and numbers have no emotion. Bettman's argument from the start was that the league was in financial trouble.

The numbers might not have looked good, but the reason behind them did not sit well with the NHLPA. The Buffalo Sabres were in terrible shape at the time because of their owner, John Rigas, who in January 2003 was charged with bank, wire and securities fraud to the tune of several billion dollars stolen from his own public company. Players' salaries were also exceeding rational amounts, and the smaller-market teams were having difficulty retaining their core star players. Both these examples of the league being in dire straits fell onto the unsympathetic ears of NHLPA executive director Bob Goodenow, who basically said Bettman was just playing politics and using the media to gain an advantage with the public for the upcoming negotiations. The showdown had started, and the two sides were not even in the boardroom together yet.

The first salvo of meetings, though, did not involve the two head honchos of the NHL and the NHLPA. Bettman sent his big friend, deputy NHL commissioner Bill Daly, in his place, and Goodenow sent his underling, deputy director Ted Saskin, to a series of meetings in order to test each other out and see if both sides had any common ground to build on.

Bettman's right-hand man, Bill Daly, was everything Gary Bettman wasn't. Although raised in New Jersey, Daly's mother was a Saskatchewanite who loved hockey, as did his American father. Daly's team of choice was always the New York Rangers. He did not just grow up around sports, he had been involved, choosing football because of his large frame. He made it all the way to university football before giving up the sport to study law.

Daly is a hockey guy, while Bettman clearly never was; that is, until February 1993 when he became NHL commissioner. Daly's passion for hockey all through his life and his deep love of sports separated him from Bettman. Even before joining the NHL administration, Daly had been an ardent hockey fan, able to rattle off statistics about long-forgotten Stanley Cup games. Bettman, on the other hand, had to read Ken Dryden's *The Game* to get a sense of the sport when he was hired.

From the NHLPA's point of view, as one of the guys, Daly was a lot easier to deal with than Bettman, and as a result, during those meetings, the two sides seemed to get along famously. The league and the NHLPA reached common ground and avoided bringing negative attitudes to the meetings. Had Saskin and Daly been in charge of the negotiations, maybe we would have had a 2005 Stanley Cup champion, but then Goodenow and Bettman joined the discussions, and everything went to hell.

Goodenow was as stubborn, or even more, as Bettman, and the two men just did not like each other. Offers were exchanged during negotiations, and all were rejected before the ink had dried. Even the start of the 2003–04 season did nothing to cool tensions. Instead of sitting down in meeting rooms, both sides traded barbs in the press, each trying to gain public support for his cause. Bettman was effective at pleading his case, saying that the league and the teams had lost $300 million in the previous season alone. The NHLPA quickly came back in the media, saying that they looked into the owners' accounting books and discovered that Bettman was fudging his numbers. The league had, in fact, lost just $96 million and was hiding millions in revenues.

The hostilities continued past the 2004 Stanley Cup playoffs and into the summer. Hockey fans started to worry that they were going to face another lockout-shortened season when September came. Both sides had rejected each other's offers, and Bettman seemed frustrated with the whole process. "We're not even speaking the same language," he moaned.

A collective sigh went out across the hockey world when in mid-September, it was officially announced that there would be another lockout. This lockout was different, though. Both sides seemed to be miles apart, and the hopes for at least a half season were dim. The players seemed aware of this fact, and before the month of September was out, over 100 players had already signed contracts in the European leagues.

For Bettman, his main goal was to establish a salary cap. The NFL and the NBA had already done the same, and it was viewed as the only way for owners to keep costs under control. The NHL team owners could not be trusted to stop one-upping each other in their bids for the best players, so the salary cap was the only solution. The problem was that the players were unwilling to accept such a deal and had built up a nice reserve fund over the years, almost in expectation of another confrontation with Bettman since the last one in 1995.

By December 2004, the chances of the players getting back to the game seemed remote. A deal put on the table by the players with a 24-percent rollback in salaries and other concessions was flatly rejected by Bettman, who then came back with an offer all his own that was deemed an insult. The NHLPA made no more offers. If Bettman and the owners wanted to save the season, they would have to offer something to the players. It was now February 2005, and the drop-dead date was a just few days away. U.S. federal mediators forced the two sides to sit down once again in the 11th hour of negotiations. The players finally buckled and accepted the imposition of a salary cap, but now it was just a matter of coming up with a number. They held all-night meetings, but

Bettman and Goodenow could not agree on a figure. The season was done.

"It is my sad duty to announce that because a solution has not yet been attained, it is no longer practical to conduct even an abbreviated season. Accordingly, I have no choice but to announce the formal cancellation of play," said Bettman at a press conference.

Many Saturdays came and went without hockey, and fans were getting desperate for their fix. In Canada, talk of revolution was not far off if the NHL did not get its act together. For one group of fans, the prospect of not having a Stanley Cup playoff was just too much to bear, so they decided to do something about it. After all, the original intention of Lord Stanley was to promote hockey for everyone to enjoy, not just a bunch of billionaire owners and their multi-millionaire employees.

A long time ago, in a tiny shop in London, England, a silversmith hammered out a glorious-looking trophy commissioned by then governor general of the Dominion of Canada, Lord Stanley of Preston (1888–93). Lord Stanley decreed that said trophy was to be named the "Dominion Hockey Challenge Cup" and was to be awarded to the top amateur team in Canada, to be decided by the acceptance of a challenge from another team.

Lord Stanley's five point rules for the awarding of the cup were simple enough:

1. The winners shall return the Cup in good order when required by the trustees so that it may be handed over to any other team which may win it.

2. Each winning team, at its own expense, may have the club name and year engraved on a silver ring fitted on the Cup.

3. The Cup shall remain a challenge cup, and should not become the property of one team, even if won more than once.

4. The trustees shall maintain absolute authority in all situations or disputes over the winner of the Cup.

5. If one of the existing trustees resigns or drops out, the remaining trustee shall nominate a substitute.

These rules were set in stone and followed as gospel for many years. But as time went on and the face of hockey changed along with North America, the awarding of the Cup changed as well. It was this original decree, and especially the third part, that many fans during the 2004–05 lockout focused on in their drive to wrestle the Cup from Bettman's hand because as Lord Stanley had said, "The Cup shall remain a challenge cup."

So when Gary Bettman announced in February 2005 that the league and the players could not come to an agreement, a group of Toronto beer league hockey players banded together and sought out the advice of lawyer Tim Gilbert.

"We kind of felt that, given [the NHL] acknowledged that there's a trust, and the trustees are the ones who have responsibility to administer the trust, we can't bind their hands and tell them exactly what to do," said Gilbert, who led the case for the recreational players. "But they have to exercise their duties in the best interests of the original purpose of the trust, which was to promote hockey."

So the beer leaguers and their lawyer took up the challenge and filed a claim with the Ontario Supreme Court, and in 2006, they won. Sort of. The decision gave the Stanley Cup trustees the opportunity—but not the obligation—to "award the Stanley Cup to a non-NHL team in any year in which the NHL fails to organize a competition to determine a Stanley Cup winner."

This decision, however pleasing for beer leaguers across Canada and the United States who dreamed of lifting the Cup since they were kids, was completely in the NHL's favor. The board of trustees of the Stanley Cup would never hand over the Cup to another league other than the NHL.

"The chances of both Brian (O'Neil) and I agreeing that it should go to any group that plays for it, I wouldn't hold your breath," said fellow trustee Ian (Scotty) Morrison in a *National Post* interview. Morrison also serves on the board for the Hockey Hall of Fame.

But the legal battle did accomplish one amazing thing. It got the NHL to admit that it was not the owner of the Stanley Cup! And the league agreed to donate $500,000 to a program run by Hockey Canada to promote the game to young women and underprivileged children.

So despite a legal battle and a stunning admission from the league, Lord Stanley's Cup has not been out of the NHL's control since 1926. The last non-NHL team to win the Cup was the 1925 Victoria Cougars of the Western Canadian Hockey League.

The cancellation of the hockey season, as well as being the first time the Cup was not handed out since 1919, angered a lot of the players as they couldn't understand what they were fighting for in the first place. The war was supposed to be about what was fair for the players and for the league, but it had turned into a war of personalities.

Goodenow and Bettman had greatly disliked each other from the start, and the whole process seemed like a charade. As a result, NHLPA president Trevor Linden and deputy director Ted Saskin took over negotiations, and by July 2005, they had signed a new collective bargaining agreement that next came due in September 2012. Although it was a relief to have a new contract, the season was dead, and the Stanley Cup sat in a case at the Hockey Hall of Fame. That shame on hockey can never be forgotten because it is engraved on Lord Stanley's mug: "2004–05 Season Not Played."

As for Bob Goodenow, his handling of the lockout was seen as a complete failure, letting his personality get in the way of negotiations and the good of the players. On July 25, 2005, he called a news conference and publicly stepped down from his post as executive director of the NHLPA and handed the reins over to Ted Saskin. The change in leadership did not end the troubles for the NHLPA, though.

The crowning of Ted Saskin was not looked upon favorably by a group of players led by grumpy old man Chris Chelios. Their objection was mainly targeted against Saskin's $2-million salary. To make matters worse, in 2007, Saskin was accused of having hacked into the emails of players. In May 2007, he was fired. Then Paul Kelly was hired as the executive director of the NHLPA, but just two years later, he too was pushed out amid questions about his friendly ties to the NHL executives.

The NHLPA was in need of some real leadership, and fast. There was a brief time when a man named Ian Penny had taken over from Paul Kelly, but Penny also got caught up in the fighting, like a Looney Tunes fight that rolls along and sweeps up everything in its way. He lasted just three months.

Then came Donald Fehr, a man who had spent a career pulling money out of the hands of sports team owners. From 1983 to 2009, he was the head of the Major League Baseball Players Association (MLBPA) and was responsible for increasing players' salaries from an average of about $250,000 to $3 million. Fehr was born to extract money from rich old men. He presided over a two-day baseball strike in 1985 followed by a 32-day lockout in 1990 and a seven-month strike in 1994–95 that wiped out the World Series for the first time in 90 years. Although the strikes were costly, what followed in baseball has been 16 years of labor peace between the owners and the players, and the game has profited because of it.

Seeing Fehr's successful track record, the NHLPA sought him out the moment it was made public that he was leaving baseball. Fehr was brought in as a consultant at first, after Ian Penny was fired, then he was officially crowned the new executive director of the NHLPA in December 2010, and he made his directives clear from the start.

During a press conference announcing his new position as NHLPA boss, Fehr discussed the keys to collective bargaining. "What goes right along with this is educating the membership at the same time as I educate myself as to what those issues are, what's important about them, how various things affect the players and then additionally what changes in the agreement—either that we might propose or that the commissioner's office might propose—could affect them," said Fehr. "Then to work with the players to identify individuals who are willing to and whom the rest of the players would like to serve on their negotiating committees moving forward. That's an awful lot of work."

Gary Bettman had to face a man on the other side of the table that had lived and breathed contract negotiations since 1983, taking on some of the richest and most stubborn team owners in the business. Fehr is Gary Bettman's exact opposite. Bettman was hired to get and keep as much of the hockey money as possible, and Fehr spent most of his life trying to get as much money from the owners as possible. Fehr knew a bit about the game of hockey, but he was a lawyer, and the art of contract negotiations was his life. The players tangled with Gary Bettman in 2004–05 and ultimately lost, giving in to a salary cap and having an entire season cancelled. This time around, Donald Fehr was on the players' side, and they could not lose.

Chapter Nine

Into the Future

After the 2005 lockout, Gary Bettman boasted that the game was now better than ever. Eighteen-year-old superstar-in-the-making Sidney Crosby had joined the league, Alexander Ovechkin was tearing it up in Washington and a little tinkering with the rules had made the game seem faster with a whole bunch of scoring. For a while, the game truly was glorious. Mario Lemieux briefly came out of retirement (again!) to play a few games with "Sid the Kid." Hockey seemed as though it was fun again, like in the 1980s, when a young group of players in Edmonton electrified the league. Gary Bettman was looking like a genius.

The lockout put an end to the ever-expanding goaltenders, whose sleek frames had been hidden under layers of protective padding that made them look like sumo wrestlers. Goalie equipment was reduced by 11 percent, allowing more open space for shooters to target. Goaltenders were further restricted when the league installed a new trapezoid area behind the goal line where they were not allowed to touch the puck. If they did, they received a two-minute penalty.

The new rule was intended to stop goaltenders like Martin Brodeur from leaving the net to play the puck in a dump-and-chase scenario, allowing the opposing team a chance at maintaining the zone. Goaltenders such as Brodeur had become so adept at playing the puck that it was like having another defenseman on the ice, which slowed down the game and reduced scoring.

Another adjustment to the rules was slight, but it helped to speed up the game. A new rule stated that when a team iced the puck, no line changes could be made. This left a tired and out-of-breath line on the ice, while the opposing team could send out fresh reinforcements. Before, if a team iced the puck, they were allowed to make a line change. The rule also put an end to the annoying commercials that always followed an icing call. As a result, games were faster, and scoring chances increased.

Gary Bettman was on a roll and continued to make changes. He even messed with the dimensions of the zones on the ice, pushing the blue lines four feet closer to the center red line in order to encourage more offensive play, particularly on the power play. Bettman's biggest success in increasing the flow of the game came with two simple rule changes. Before the 2005–06 season, if a player behind the defensive blue line made a pass to a forward on the opposite side of the red line, it was called as a two-line pass, and the play was whistled dead. For the new NHL season, the league basically removed the red line, which allowed players to make long-stretch passes, leading to more breakaways on goaltenders.

Another helpful way the league created a better flow to the game was to bring in the "tag-up" rule that permits play to continue "if offensive players who preceded the puck into the zone return to the blue line and 'tag' it."

NHL officials were also asked to crack down on interference, hooking and holding infractions. In the old NHL, a player could grab onto another player from behind with his stick and almost get pulled along with the player, with no calls from the referee. But under the new NHL, if a player tapped another player with his stick at waist height, he would sit in the box for two minutes.

The 2005 lockout also caused the death of the NHL tie game. Prior to the lockout, if two teams failed to score in the five minutes of overtime during the regular season, the game was deemed a tie. As of October 2005, ties no longer existed. If a game went into overtime, both teams were allowed only four skaters up front instead of five, in order to create more open ice. However, if at the end of the five minutes, no one had scored, the game would go into a shootout. Coaches from each team would then select three players to go one-on-one against the goaltenders, and the team with the most goals after the six shooters played won the game. If no player scored, or if both teams were even after six shooters, the game would go into a "sudden death" shootout with both teams sending out one player to attempt to score until the stalemate was broken and a winner declared.

The shootout was hailed by fans. The most exciting moment in hockey has always been when a penalty shot is called, so why not rid the league of the boring tie and end the game with a series of white-knuckle breakaways? The first NHL regular-season shootout occurred between the Ottawa Senators and the Toronto Maple Leafs on October 5, 2005. After battling to a 2–2 tie, and overtime solving nothing, the shootout started off with the Senators captain Daniel Alfredsson.

Every single person in the arena that night got to their feet and cheered wildly. Alfredsson put himself in the history books by scoring on Toronto goalie Ed Belfour with a quick wrist shot, low goal side, and putting Ottawa ahead. The goal was followed by a miss from Toronto's Jason Allison. The Senators Dany Heatley put Ottawa in a comfortable spot, scoring on his attempt, then the Leafs Eric Lindros missed his attempt on Sens goaltender Dominic Hasek to put an end to the first shootout.

But today, after more than seven seasons of NHL shootouts, the game has begun to lose some of its excitement. Goaltenders hate having the fate of important games put solely on their shoulders, and hockey purists want a return to the old tie system or have overtime continue until there is a winner, as in the playoffs. Critics also have a problem with a team receiving a single point for losing a game. When the game goes into overtime, both teams are automatically given a single point, and an additional point goes to the winner of the shootout. This point system has made the NHL standings a lot closer and muddied the distinction between the best and worst teams.

Sports for all of history has been about a winner and a loser. The NHL shootout system rewards teams for almost winning, and as a result, many critics have been calling for its end. Mark Sutcliffe of the *Ottawa Citizen* wrote a long feature piece in the newspaper after a particularly strange shootout attempt by the Senators Kaspars Daugavins on Boston Bruins goalie Tuukka Rask during the 2012–13 lockout-shortened season. The Senators forward held the puck on the ice with the tip of his stick blade and skated down the ice stickhandling like a ringette player before trying a "spin-o-rama" on Rask that failed to score. This move got Sutcliffe thinking about getting rid of the shootout:

> *NHL games should continue until there's a winner, just like papal conclaves, baseball and basketball games and, hey, NHL playoff games. Hockey players are some of the best conditioned athletes in the world. They can handle more than five minutes of extra play.*
>
> *Most overtime games are decided pretty quickly anyway.*
>
> *The occasional lengthy overtime game would be entertaining for the fans who chose to hang around. It would mean teams would have to put players who normally get three minutes of ice time to better use. And it would be a prouder and nobler way of deciding a game, more consistent with hockey's character, than a bunch of breakaways.*

Although Gary Bettman was largely praised for his changes at first, the negative effects of those changes soon became apparent. Once again, the honeymoon phase was over for Bettman.

The rule changes opened up the game, created a better flow and allowed for more scoring, but that openness was not necessarily a good thing. Because the game was moving faster, players were suffering more injuries. Although Bettman has often said he takes player safety seriously, he has had to be on both sides of the issue when it comes to violence on the ice. Prior to Bettman's arrival, the league had installed the instigator rule, which adds an extra two minutes to the penalty of the player who starts a fight. Before the installation of the instigator rule, the hockey enforcer was the one who meted out punishment on the ice according to the fighting code. So, basically, if a player went after a star or was on the ice with intent to injure, then it was the enforcer's job to put that player back in line with a few fists to the face.

However, the rule had a few unintended consequences, most notably, the staged fight. When there is cause to fight, and both teams want to avoid the extra two-minute penalty, the coaches will send out their two enforcers and get them to drop their gloves at the same time. With this, the role of punishing bad hockey players with on-ice justice disappeared, and hockey purists hated it.

Don Cherry, a one-time enforcer, gave his vocal opinion on the subject, referring to Pittsburgh Penguins Matt Cooke's cheap shot hit to the head of the Bruins Marc Savard. "Back in the 1970s, if a guy did that, he wouldn't finish in the game," said Cherry. "Can you imagine in your wildest dreams somebody doing that to (Wayne) Gretzky when (Marty) McSorley and (Dave) Semenko was on the club? It would never happen because we didn't have the instigator rule like they have now.... It's not lack of respect, it's lack of fear.... If you ever did it with my team, you wouldn't finish the game."

Despite protests from coaches, players and general managers, Gary Bettman remained steadfast in his belief that policing the game was the responsibility of the league and not the tough guys. Bettman believed in the rule so much that he strengthened it in 2005: "A player who instigates a fight in the final five minutes of a game will receive a game misconduct and an automatic one-game suspension. The length of suspension would double for each additional incident. As well, the player's Coach will be fined $10,000—a fine that would double for each such incident."

The rule took away players' ability to self-regulate, and the role of the enforcer began to slowly fade away. As a result, players who played dirty began to rule the league. Bettman might have reduced fighting, but the amount of stick-related injuries increased markedly, as did the infamous head shots that have ended too many careers.

Without the constant fear of a Dave Semenko or a Georges Laraque on the ice to make the aggressors answer for their actions, the league's superstars have become prime targets. Gary Bettman's poster boy Sidney Crosby was not even immune. At the 2011 Winter Classic, the NHL premiere event broadcast across the United States and Canada, it was Crosby's Penguins versus the Washington Capitals. On an innocent play, when Crosby did not even have the puck, the Capitals Dave Steckel blindsided Crosby with an elbow to the head, knocking him to the ice. Steckel received no suspensions or fines as the hit was deemed an unfortunate byproduct of a "hockey play." However, if you review the incident on video, there is little doubt that Steckel intended to hit Crosby. Steckel is a professional who knows what he is doing and where he is on the ice at all times, and without fear of retribution, he was able to get away with the hit that eventually led to Crosby missing the rest of the season.

The Crosby hit is just one of a host of suspect hits that the league has passed over and not taken affirmative action on, and it continues to this day with (at the time of this writing) several players already having been suspended in just the first round of the 2013 Stanley Cup playoffs. But is the answer to allow fighting in order to stop these types of players from killing someone on the ice? Although having fighters hand out justice on the ice might be a way to curb the cheap-shot artists of the league, there are also consequences for the fighters themselves. That became more apparent with the deaths of noted tough guys Bob Probert, Rick Rypien, Derek Boogaard and Wade Belak.

The life of an NHL fighter is not easy. He wakes up every morning knowing that he might have to punch another human being in the face during a game that night. When he gets to the rink, he knows his teammates are counting on him to fight, he knows the coaches are expecting him to drop his gloves, and when he goes to bed later that night, he knows that come next game, he will have to do it all over again. Now, although they have fallen into the category of fighter during their careers, most of those players did not start out in hockey that way, and with each fight they get into, it seems to eat away at their souls.

"Knowing that inner battle that you have to do this job, but I've seen it torn [*sic*] guys apart," said retired fighter Nick Kypreos, whose career ended because of a concussion he received during a fight.

"[The] inner battle between fighting and what it does to and what it does for the people around you; wives, children, parents. You know, it's not a glamorous thing, and some guys really have trouble with it."

Bob Probert battled drugs and alcohol his entire professional career, as did enforcer Derek Boogaard, and both men died as a result of the lifestyle they lived. Along with the drug problems came bouts of severe depression that reduced these once-towering figures of strength to empty shells. It is an image that is not pretty, and it's one that the NHL has been slow to react to, even with the deaths of these high-profile players. While the league and Bettman play politics, science has recently brought some interesting facts to light, specifically in the cases of Boogaard and Probert.

After their deaths, autopsies showed that both men had suffered from a degenerative brain disease called chronic traumatic encephalopathy (CTE). The disease is progressive and occurs in people who suffer repeated trauma to the head. Individuals with the disease show symptoms of dementia, memory loss, aggression, confusion and depression, all of which were experienced by Boogaard, Rypien, Belak and Probert. But despite all the medical evidence, Bettman and the league have distanced themselves from the issue.

When Bettman was told that the brains of Boogaard and Probert showed signs of CTE, he made a comment:

> *We don't know everything that went on in their lives. We don't know what else they had in common, if anything. So, I think when you look at the fact that the medical community has only been dealing with the issue of concussions in the way that they have for probably the last few decades, and if you look at our history starting in 1997 and we've been across all fronts— whether it's the study, the working groups, baseline testing, diagnosis and return-to-play protocols, rule changes, the creation of the Department of Player Safety—we've been doing lots and lots and we'll continue to do lots and lots. But, there are no easy answers yet. And, I think it's unfortunate if people use tragedies to jump to conclusions that probably at this stage aren't supported.*

Then Bettman further distanced himself from the issue, saying officially, and in a vague way, "Maybe it is [dangerous] and maybe it's not. You don't know that for a fact and it's something we continue to monitor. The level of concussions from fighting is not rising, it's constant, so it's not an increasing problem. But, it is something we'll continue to monitor."

While Bettman continues to dance around the problems of the league, the NHL has never been more profitable, and money, at the end of the day, is what makes him believe he has done a good job. For the 2011–12 season, league revenues hit a historic high of over $3 billion, and a record number of people paid (or got tickets through work) to go through the turnstiles and watch their favorite teams. Sure, ticket prices are higher, lockouts have scarred the league and the product on the ice has slowed down, but people are still showing up.

It's not as though everyone hates Gary Bettman. The Winter Classic and the Heritage Classic have given the NHL a marquee event in mid-season and helped attract new attention to the league. (Though in Canada, it's not that hard to sell the game. Canadians do that on their own, making Bettman's job in that country easy.) He has secured a major television deal and put the lowly Atlanta Thrashers out of their misery and moved them to Winnipeg, where they are greatly appreciated. He has also kept the Ottawa Senators, the Edmonton Oilers, the Dallas Stars, the Buffalo Sabres and the St. Louis Blues all from going bankrupt. He has made the rich owners even richer, and the players likewise, and kept hockey moving forward. He hasn't always moved in the right direction or traveled on a smooth road, but say what you will about the man, he gets results.

Yet for all the changes, hockey lags behind the other big sports and will likely never get out of their shadow. The hardest part of Bettman's journey has been convincing Americans to embrace the sport as passionately as Canadians, especially when Americans only discovered the game in recent years. Hockey is Canada's game, like it or not, but Bettman will never stop trying to get the regular American Joe Blow to care about what is happening in the NHL. He has a long way to go. As proof, imagine Sidney Crosby or Wayne Gretzky (in his prime) walking down the street in downtown Dallas, Texas, today; how many people would stop him to get an autograph? One or two, and most likely they would be Canadian tourists. Now put those two players on any street in any town in Canada, and imagine how they would be treated. Gary Bettman would love nothing more than to have the Canadian reaction on the streets of Dallas.

As for how Bettman is received on the street, he couldn't care less. What matters to him are results. However, it was hard for him not to show his surprise when he walked out onto the ice at the end of the 2012 playoffs to hand the Los Angeles Kings their first Stanley Cup and no one booed. No one jeered. No one tossed their $8 beer at him. But after another lockout that took away half of the 2012–13 season, I would imagine that Bettman will not be very well received by the next city he visits to present the Cup. You can almost guarantee that if a Canadian team is in the final, Bettman will be booed mercilessly. And that would be just fine with him. It means he is doing his job.

Chapter Ten

Timeline

1943

- NHL president Frank Calder dies, leaving the office of the president vacant for the first time since the league was created in 1917.

- Red Dutton runs the league as managing director until 1945, when he takes over as president.

1946

- Red Dutton steps down and hands over the title to his assistant, Clarence Campbell.

1967

- Clarence Campbell oversees the expansion of the NHL from the "Original Six" teams to 12 in total.

1970s

- Rival professional league the World Hockey Association starts up in Quebec City, Edmonton and San Francisco, and many NHL players defect for better money.

- Clarence Campbell steps down as NHL president in 1977. American-born John Ziegler takes over.

1990s

- New teams enter the NHL:

  San Jose Sharks (1991)

  Ottawa Senators (1992)

  Tampa Bay Lightning (1992)

  Anaheim Mighty Ducks (1993)

  Dallas Stars (1993)

  Florida Panthers (1993)

  Colorado Avalanche (1995)

  Phoenix Coyotes (1996)

  Carolina Hurricanes (1997)

  Nashville Predators (1998)

  Atlanta Thrashers (1999)

- The Minnesota North Stars, the Quebec Nordiques, the Winnipeg Jets and the Hartford Whalers fold.

1991

- Alan Eagleson is thrown out of his position as executive director of the National Hockey League Players Association after it was revealed he was a little too comfortable with the owners and was involved in embezzling player pension funds for years.

1992

- With Bob Goodenow as leader of the players' union, a 10-day strike starts just before the end of the playoffs. The strike wins the players major perks and increase in revenue. As a result of the strike, the NHL owners fire president John Ziegler and appoint Gil Stein as interim leader.

1993

- On February 1, the NHL announces the hiring of former New York lawyer and NBA employee Gary Bettman as the league's commissioner. He is brought on to tackle labor unrest, to grow the game in the United States and to modernize the league into a proper corporation.

- Bettman hands out a 21-game suspension to Washington Capitals forward Dale Hunter for his vicious shot on New York Islanders star Pierre Turgeon.

- Bettman presents his first Stanley Cup to the Montreal Canadiens. No one boos.

1994

- The New York Rangers win the Stanley Cup. Bettman receives polite applause at the presentation ceremony.

- After months of trying to find common ground in the new collective bargaining agreement (CBA), the league and the players' union fail to come to terms, and the NHL is forced into locking out its workforce.

- Bettman signs a multimillion-dollar television contract with the Fox Network, putting hockey into the homes of millions more Americans.

1994–2000

- Season goals per game drop per year—in 1994, the top-scoring Detroit Red Wings had 356 goals combined compared with the top-scoring Toronto Maple Leafs in 1999, who had 268 combined goals.

1995

- After late-night marathon contract negotiations, the NHL and the NHLPA come to an agreement in the last hour to announce the end to contract talks and the start of the season. It is the first time since 1941–42 that an NHL season lasts only 48 games, and the Leafs won the Cup that year. The contract lasts until September 2004.

- The New Jersey Devils win the Stanley Cup. Bettman is booed by the crowd as his name is announced.

1996

- The FoxTrax Puck is introduced at the NHL All-Star game. Technology inside the puck allows televisions to convert the information into a glowing, colored comet that shoots across the screen like a wishing star whenever a player slaps the puck. It is used in American television until 1998. Its demise brought many cheers.

1997

- At the Civic Arena in Pittsburgh, Gary Bettman is booed when presenting at the NHL entry draft.

2000

- The Columbus Blue Jackets and the Minnesota Wild join the NHL.

November 2003

- The NHL puts on the first Heritage Classic in Edmonton, Alberta. It is a regular-season NHL game played outdoors between the Montreal Canadiens and the Edmonton Oilers. Over 57,000 people sit outside in the freezing cold to watch the event. An exhibition game between star legends of the Canadiens and the Oilers is held prior to the "real" game. Wayne Gretzky returns to Edmonton wearing his old number 99 for the first time since his August 1988 trade to the Los Angeles Kings.

2004

• With NHL teams in financial trouble, players' salaries reaching ridiculous heights and the coming of contract negotiations, the NHL season is cancelled when the NHLPA and the league cannot agree to a new deal. The biggest stumbling block for the players is the addition of a salary cap. This is the first time since 1919 that the Stanley Cup is not awarded. (The 1919 Stanley Cup final between the Montreal Canadiens and the Seattle Metropolitans was cancelled as a result of the worldwide Spanish influenza epidemic.)

• Gary Bettman's salary: $3.7 million.

2005

• The league and the NHLPA finally come together to resolve their differences in July and sign a new contract that will come up for renewal in September 2012. (Sense a pattern?)

• The Pittsburgh Penguins win the Sidney Crosby sweepstakes, selecting the most highly touted player since Wayne Gretzky came to hockey.

2005–06

• NHL hockey returns to action for the season. Bettman is loudly booed when announcing his congratulations to the Carolina Hurricanes in their victory over the Edmonton Oilers for the Cup. Had the final game been in Edmonton, a mob might have formed.

• After several years on the ABC and ESPN networks in the U.S., NHL hockey is moved over to the Outdoor Life Network (OLN) by Bettman. OLN then becomes Versus and is later purchased by NBC Universal.

2008

• The first NHL Winter Classic, an outdoor game between the Pittsburgh Penguins and the Buffalo Sabres. Sidney Crosby wins the game for the Penguins in the shootout. A record 71,217 fans turn up to see the game.

2010

• The Boston Bruins beat the Vancouver Canucks in the seventh game of the playoffs before a Vancouver crowd. Bettman is mercilessly booed by angry fans and even has several full beer cups tossed at him. (They must have been really angry, because why else would someone toss away a $10 beer?)

2011

• The Winnipeg Jets return to the NHL.

2012

• Gary Bettman's salary: $7.98 million! His rank, in annual salary, when compared to the top-earning NHL players:

1. Alex Ovechkin: $9,538,462

2. Evgeni Malkin: $8,700,000

3. Sidney Crosby: $8,700,000

4. Eric Staal: $8,250,000

5. Gary Bettman: $7,980,000

6. Shea Weber: $7,857,143

7. Rick Nash: $7,800,000

8. Vincent Lecavalier: $7,727,273

9. Zach Parise: $7,538,462

10. Ryan Suter: $7,538,462

2012–13

• The NHL season is once again put on hold while the league and the NHLPA work out their contractual differences.

January 2013

• Donald Fehr, executive director of the NHLPA, and Gary Bettman reach an agreement on the CBA. Hockey returns for a shortened 48-game schedule.

Gary Bettman and Pop Culture

Gary Bettman Humor

As the leader of the NHL, you are bound to be the butt of some jokes. It happens to the best leaders, but when you are a short, New York City lawyer whom many people picture with a very large chip on his shoulder, you are going to be the target of more than your fair share of biting humor. Adding fuel to the fire, Gary Bettman did not help his cause by being the face of the league through three lockouts in 20 years, one of them leading to the complete cancellation of league play for one full season. That lockout really made Gary Bettman the target of much off-color humor and jokes that make some people uncomfortable.

Here are a few Gary Bettman jokes that have circled the pubs, restaurants, dressing rooms and homes of the players more than once during Bettman's tenure as NHL commissioner. (If you are connected to the Internet and want a chuckle,

I strongly suggest you to search for "Gary Bettman jokes" and then check out the images. The creators of Internet memes love Bettman.)

New Toy

Did you hear about the new action-figure doll called "Negotiation Bettman"? It comes with all the players' stuff.

Commissioner Genealogy

(This joke plays to the common theme of "diminishment" in humor.)

A man enters a bar and orders a drink.

The bar has a robot bartender. The robot serves the man a perfectly prepared cocktail and then asks him, "What's your IQ?"

The man replies, "150."

The robot proceeds to make conversation about global warming issues, quantum physics, spirituality, biochemistry, environmental interconnectedness, string theory, nano-technology and sexual proclivities.

The customer is quite impressed and thinks to himself, "This is really cool." He decides to test the robot. He walks out of the bar, turns around and comes back in for another drink.

Again, the robot serves him a perfectly prepared drink and asks him, "What's your IQ?"

The man responds, "About 100."

Immediately, the robot starts talking, but this time about football, Bathurst1000, cricket, super-models, favorite fast foods, guns and women's breasts.

Really impressed, the man leaves the bar and decides to give the robot one last test.

When he returns, the robot serves him and then asks, "What's your IQ?"

The man replies, "Er, 50, I think."

And the robot says real slowly, "Are...you... related...to...Gary...Bettman?"

Q: How does Gary Bettman change a light bulb?

A: He holds it in the air, and the world revolves around him.

Shortest book ever: *How to Win Friends and Influence People*, by Gary Bettman.

Most unnecessary book ever: *The Art of Negotiations*, by Gary Bettman.

Message on Bettman's Answering Machine

"Hi! This is Gary! If you're my kids, I already sent the money. If you're an owner, settle this thing about the money. If you're the NHLPA, I don't have enough money. If you're my friends, you owe me money. If you're my wife, don't worry—I have plenty of money."

Lock up Your Children

Writer Luke Gordon Field wrote a hilarious fake news article on his website (thebeaverton.com) about the lockout, but instead of Bettman locking out the players, Bettman has locked his children out of the house. "Citing rising allowance costs, Bettman locks his children out of the house," reads the headline. The lead paragraph is pure Gary Bettman comedy gold: "Westchester, CT: Saying his household could no longer keep up with the dramatic increase in money being paid toward their allowance, embattled NHL commissioner Gary Bettman took the bold step of locking his children, Brittany (5), Lauren (7) and Jordan (9), out of their suburban Connecticut home."

Bye-bye, Bettman

The website www.garybettmansucks.com is a wonderful tribute to the NHL commissioner's public relations skills. There are also several Facebook group pages with such titles as "Fire Bettman" or "Bettman Must Go!" or some other play on words, all with the intention of getting rid of Bettman.

Bettman and God

(A classic play on personality)

Gary Bettman, Mario Lemieux and Steve Yzerman all die and meet in heaven. God is sitting in his chair waiting for them. God says to the three legends, "Gentleman, before I let you in, you must tell me what you believe. Mario, we'll start with you. In what do you believe?"

"I believe hockey is the greatest thing in the world and the best sport in history," replies Lemieux.

To that, God says, "Take the seat to my left." God then turns to Steve Yzerman and says, "Steven, in what do you believe?"

To which Yzerman replies, "I believe that to be the best, you've got to give every ounce you've got!"

God says to Steve, "Take the seat to my right."

God then turns to the NHL commissioner and says, "Gary, tell me, what do you believe?"

To which Bettman replies, "I believe you are sitting in my seat."

Saving a Life Is Bad

In the middle of lockout negotiations, Gary Bettman falls into a freezing lake in Ontario while taking a walk during a break from negotiations. Three young boys rescue Bettman from drowning. He is so grateful that he tells the boys, "I'll give you anything you want for saving my life! Just name it!"

The first boy thinks for a second and then says, "I'd like a Ferrari, red, and a million dollars."

"No problem! You will have what you want," says Bettman. "What about you, little boy?" he asks the second boy.

"I'd like to play hockey with Wayne Gretzky, Sidney Crosby and Martin Brodeur," says the second boy.

"Sure. That I can do, no problem!" says Bettman. "How about you, my little hero?"

"I'd like a motorized wheelchair," replies the third boy.

"Why would you need a wheelchair?" asks Bettman. "You look pretty healthy to me."

"Because," replies the boy, "I'll need a wheelchair when my dad finds out I saved Gary Bettman from drowning, and the lockout is going to continue now."

Betting on Bettman

Gary Bettman has been involved in three NHL lockouts in 20 years—now known as the "Gary Bettman Hat Trick."

Character Flaw

(Bettman in the media and in contract negotiations has always been reported to be a man who never deviates from his way of thinking, even if he might be wrong.)

Three men are sentenced to death and brought to face their fate. The executioner says to the first man, "You have a choice: you may die by either lethal injection or electric chair."

The man chooses lethal injection. The injection is given, and the man dies.

The second man is offered the same choice. He selects the electric chair. The executioner pulls the switch, but nothing happens. He tries again. Again nothing happens.

"Well," the executioner says, "according to our laws, you've made your choice and the punishment was administered, so we are done. You are free to go." The man walks away free.

Then the executioner asks the third man, who just happens to be NHL commissioner Gary Bettman, the same question: "Lethal injection or electric chair?"

"I think lethal injection," replies Bettman. "The electric chair is obviously broken."

Money, Money, Money

(Fair or not, Gary Bettman has always been portrayed as a money man. Hockey was not in his blood, and therefore he never earned the respect of the players. This joke plays on Bettman's obsession with the numbers and money.)

A boy is playing with a penny when it gets stuck in his throat and he starts to choke. His mother runs into the street calling for help, and a man passing by offers his assistance. The man grabs hold of the boy, puts his mouth over the boy's mouth and skillfully sucks out the penny.

"Thank you, doctor!" says the woman. "Did you learn that in medical school?"

"Oh, I'm not a doctor," replies the man. "I'm the NHL commissioner."

Poor, Poor Bettman

A traffic cop finds Gary Bettman on the highway in a distressed state. With no money to pay his lawyers, and convinced that his family all hate him, Bettman threatens to douse his clothes in gasoline and set himself on fire.

A passerby notices that the traffic cop is stopping vehicles, and he asks the cop what is going on.

The cop explains that because he feels sorry for the NHL commissioner, he is going from car to car asking for donations.

"How much have you collected so far?" asks the passerby.

"About 10 gallons."

Cold Out?

(This one must be popular with the players' union.)

Two professional hockey players meet on the street.

The first player exclaims, "Man, it was cold this morning!"

"How cold was it?" asks the other player.

"I don't know exactly what the temperature was, but I saw Gary Bettman and the team owners with their hands in their own pockets."

Birds of a Feather

(This joke involves one of Gary Bettman's strongest supporters among the ownership group in the NHL and one of the most hardline.)

Boston Bruins owner Jeremy Jacobs suddenly dies. His heartbroken widow organizes an intimate funeral and invites everyone he knew. When the service is over, she asks his three closest friends to place an offering in the casket, as it is a family tradition.

Moved by her suffering, the first friend, another NHL owner, gently deposits $1000 in the coffin.

Wiping his tears away, the second friend, the Bruins general manager, puts $1500 on his pillow.

His third friend, Gary Bettman, writes out a check for $4500, puts it in the casket and pockets the cash.

I'm Walking Here!

(This is one of the meaner jokes out there, which makes it funnier for some reason.)

A hockey fan is driving home from work and sees a local priest walking on the side of the road. He stops and offers the priest a lift. The priest thanks him kindly, and together they proceed to the church to drop the priest off.

On the way there, they pass a man walking his dog on the other side of the road. On closer inspection, the driver sees that the man is NHL commissioner Gary Bettman. Now, the driver hates the NHL boss and suddenly feels an uncontrollable urge to run his car into him. The driver slams his foot down on the accelerator and tries to hit Bettman. At the last second, Bettman jumps out of the way. Although the driver of the car hears a loud thump, he is sure he has missed Bettman.

The hockey fan and the priest continue to the church in silence, and as the hockey fan pulls up to the curb, he says, "Look, Father, I'm really sorry about that incident back there. I don't know what came over me. Can you ever forgive me, Father?"

The priest replies, "Of course I can forgive you, my son. I got him with the car door."

Giddy Up!

(This one plays on the common jokes about the NHL commissioner's smaller frame.)

During a break from lockout talks, Gary Bettman goes on a brief vacation and has a terrible experience riding a horse. For no apparent reason, the beast starts to get out of control. It becomes wild and angry. Bettman tries desperately to hang onto the reins, but the horse is so unpredictable that Bettman is eventually thrown off. As he falls, his foot gets caught in the stirrup, and his head bounces repeatedly on the ground with the horse refusing to stop or even slow down.

Finally, Bettman is saved when the mall security guard unplugs the machine.

Out Driving

I rear ended Gary Bettman with my car today. He got out and said, "I am not happy!"

I replied, "Well, then, which dwarf are you?"

In Hell

(You know people really care when they put you in a joke about hell.)

A man dies and is taken to his place of eternal torment by the devil.

As he passes sulfurous pits and shrieking sinners, he sees a man he recognizes as Gary Bettman snuggling up to a beautiful woman.

"That's unfair!" the man cries. "I have to roast for all eternity, and Gary Bettman gets to spend it with a gorgeous woman!"

"Shut up!" barks the devil, jabbing the man with his pitchfork. "Who are you to question that woman's punishment?"

A Father's Lesson

"My boy," says Gary Bettman to his son, who is just starting out as a lawyer, "if you are to succeed in business, there are two things that are vitally important to remember: honesty and foresight."

"What exactly do you mean by *honesty*, Dad?" asks the son.

"No matter what happens," replies Bettman, "always keep your word once you have given it."

"And *foresight*?" asks the young man.

"Never give your word in the first place."

In the Movies

Not only is Gary Bettman the target of joke writers, but he has also been lampooned on the big screen in the 2006 Canadian hit movie, *Bon Cop, Bad Cop*, starring Colm Feore and Patrick Huard. The film is about two cops, one French Canadian, one English Canadian, who must work together to solve a series of murders that are related to the hockey world. Although never mentioned, all the teams, players and owners parody the real NHL, even the beloved commissioner Gary Bettman, whose alter ego in the movie is named Harry Buttman.

The Buttman character is played by an actor with a striking resemblance to the NHL commissioner, down to the part in the hair, the large nose and the diminutive stature (for this the producers went a little too far as the actor is under 5 feet tall). In one scene in the movie, Harry Buttman is seen sitting in a room talking with another man via webcam, finalizing a deal to move another hockey team to the U.S. market when he is interrupted by a knock at the door. He is kidnapped at gunpoint and forced inside a duffel bag.

At the Juno's

Hatred of Bettman runs deep in Canada, so deep, in fact, that his face made an appearance at an event that had nothing to do with hockey or athletes. At the 2013 Juno Music Awards, host Michael Bublé told a joke about pop superstar Justin Bieber and was booed for doing so. Bublé then instructed the audience, "If you feel the need to boo, fine, then let's boo." Then, with a snap of his fingers, a picture of the smiling NHL commissioner appeared on a big screen, and without hesitation, the entire audience began to boo.

Can't Blame Bettman for this One

We all know by now about Gary Bettman's history with hockey and his role in the cancellation of an entire NHL season and the absence of a Stanley Cup champion in 2005. Losing an entire season is traumatic enough, but not having the Stanley Cup presented is downright tragic. It has to do with what the Cup has come to symbolize. It is a part of the hockey tradition, something every person aspires to. Even if it "belongs" to the NHL, the Cup really belongs to us all.

The Stanley Cup, unlike any other professional sports trophy, has a special meaning to all that love the game. People feel connected to it in a strange way, even if they know they will never become professional hockey players and lift it in triumph. All you need to do to understand this sentiment is to observe people when they are around the Cup. Suddenly they are all kids again, playing street hockey, pretending to be their favorite player who scores the game-winning Stanley Cup goal.

This strong connection to the Cup is why beer league players tried to sue the NHL for control of the trophy during the 2005 lockout. You can blame Gary Bettman all you want for the loss of a Cup champion in 2005, but you would be hard-pressed to find some link with the NHL commissioner and the first time the Stanley Cup was not awarded. (Unless it was his grandparents who were the first to get sick. Read on.)

Soldiers during World War I fought in some of the most disgusting environments. Night and day, they ate, slept and fought in cold, muddy trenches with rats and dead soldiers as companions. Wading through sometimes waist-high water that was contaminated with feces and urine, it was only a matter of time before soldiers started getting sick with what at first appeared to be a bad cold. As soldiers began to return home, that cold, actually the influenza virus, began to spread.

Throughout the entire world, over 21 million people died from what was called Spanish influenza. In Canada and the United States, entire communities were wiped out. In an attempt to minimize the effect of the disease, government officials closed schools, all non-essential work was halted, and people were told to avoid gathering in groups.

In only its second year, the National Hockey League in 1919 faced a major roadblock to establishing itself in North America. League-wide attendance dropped because of government warnings on posters plastered all over cities telling people to stay home. The NHL and its players were not immune to the disease, either.

At the beginning of the 1918–19 season, the NHL managed to sign up only three teams: the Ottawa Senators, the Montreal Canadiens and the Toronto Arenas. But halfway through the season, the Toronto Arenas had to withdraw from the league because of financial difficulties. This forced the NHL to start the playoffs early, with the only two remaining teams.

Before 1926, the NHL did not have sole owner-ship of the Stanley Cup. The champion of the NHL had to play the champion of the Pacific Coast Hockey Association (PCHA) for the right to be named Stanley Cup champion.

In the NHL final, the Montreal Canadiens, led by Newsy Lalonde, easily beat the Senators in the best-of-seven series in five games, to move on to play the PCHA champion, the Seattle Metropoli-tans. The only problem for this Stanley Cup final series was that it was to be played in Seattle, mean-ing that the Canadiens would have to travel across country on a train in the middle of an influenza epidemic. The players seemed to be okay when the series got underway on March 19, 1919, but as it progressed, several of the Montreal Canadiens players began to fall ill. After five games and with several players out sick, both franchises decided to call the finals a draw and not award the Cup to either team. Newsy Lalonde, Louis Berlinquette and owner Georges Kennedy all fell ill with the disease but eventually recovered. The only player who never left his bed was the Canadiens Joe Hall. Hall died in a Seattle hospital from the influenza virus.

This was the first and unfortunately not the last time the Stanley Cup was not awarded.

Bettman in the Headlines

Although he might get the odd positive headline or a weak thumbs up, Gary Bettman is not a media favorite. Here are just a few headlines taken from newspapers, websites and blogs:

Gary Bettman is Very Predictable, and Usually Lying

–Cam Charron, editorial on thescore.com

Gary Bettman's Latest Salary Revealed

–Luke Fox, sportsnet.ca (shown with a photo of Bettman with an "Oh yeah!" smirk on his face)

With Lockout Now Over, It's Time for Gary Bettman to Step Down

–Ken Campbell, *The Hockey News*

Don Cherry: Gary Bettman "Saved the Season"

–CBC.ca

Prime Minister Stephen Harper to Gary Bettman: Let NHL Stars Play in Sochi Winter Olympics

–Associated Press

Gary Bettman Is the Most Hated Man In Hockey

–Jeff Beer, canadianbusiness.com

Why Does Gary Bettman Get All the Blame?

–Ken Campbell, *The Hockey News*

NHL Commissioner Gary Bettman Gets Candid

–John Mazerolle, metronews.ca

Bettman Says Another Lockout Looms

–Ira Podell and Rachel Cohen, Associated Press

Will Bettman Bring the Nordiques Back to Quebec?

–Canadian Press

Kris Versteeg: Gary Bettman and Bill Daly Are "Cancers"

> –Bruce Garrioch, *The Ottawa Sun*

NHL lockout: Gary Bettman Enrages NHL Opinion Leaders with Verbal Attack on Journalist

> –David Staples, *The Edmonton Journal*

Bettman Tells Winnipeg Newspaper: "I Love the Players"

> –Mark Brehm, *USA Today Sports*

Predators' Colin Wilson Says Gary Bettman "Phony"

> –Paul Friesen, *Winnipeg Sun*

Disgruntled NHL Fan Confronts Bettman at News Conference

> –Josh Yohe, triblive.com

Simmons: Gary Bettman Should Be Fired After NHL Lockout

> –Steve Simmons, *Toronto Sun*

NHL Lockout: Latest Winter Classic News Proves Gary Bettman Is Wrong Man for NHL

> –Nicholas Goss, thebleacherreport.com

With a Salary Near $8 Million a Year, Is NHL Commissioner Gary Bettman Overpaid?

> –Eric McKelvie, thebleacherreport.com

NHL Boss Gary Bettman Fighting Cold War Without Obvious Exit Strategy (With Poll)

> –Iain MacIntrye, *Vancouver Sun*

Gary Bettman Remains a Stern Guy in Labor Talks

> –Helene Elliott, *Los Angeles Times*

NHL Supports Gay Athletes; Bettman: "Hockey Is for Everyone"

> –Fox News (To give credit where due, the NHL was the first major league to step up and support gay rights in sports.)

Quotations about Gary Bettman and by Gary Bettman

- Gary Bettman on his new counterpart Donald Fehr's hiring as NHLPA director in 2010: "We are pleased that the leadership position at the Players' Association has been filled, and we look forward to working with Don in his new role."

- Bettman on contract negotiations: "It takes two sides to make a deal, two sides to negotiate and two sides to make it go bad."

- Bettman after announcing the end of the 2004–05 season: "My message to the kids and our fans is hockey's a great game. There's a lot of hockey being played at all levels. Get involved, do it. We will be back, and we will be back better than ever and hopefully as soon as possible. Don't give up on the game. It's too good."

- Bettman on the Canadian hockey market: "The Canadian franchises and Canada as a market for NHL hockey has always been a priority for us."

- Bettman on the state of the game in 2005: "To use a hockey analogy, for the first time in a long while, the NHL has momentum. I'm determined to see us build upon it and grow this great game."

- Bettman on the 2005 lockout: "We made, at the time, what we thought was a fair deal. It actually turned out to be more fair than perhaps it should have been."

- Gary Bettman on his feelings for the players during the 2005 lockout: "By the way, I love the players. Nobody should think for a moment I don't."

- NHL agent Allan Walsh responding via twitter to Bettman's comments on his love for the players: "It's a good thing Gary Bettman really loves the players, otherwise we'd all be screwed."

- *Toronto Star* reporter Damien Cox on the 2005 lockout: "Intriguing that players can 'hate' Bettman so much when salaries and benefits have increased pretty much every year since he took over."

- Former head coach Barry Melrose on the 2005 lockout: "There was no reason to go through all this hell and frustration to get a deal...I think we let our game slip. It's broken right now."

- *Sports Illustrated* writer E.M. Swift on Gary Bettman after the 2005 lockout: "He had to burn the village in order to save it. Gary Bettman is my Sportsman of the Year. OK, so it doesn't make a pretty cover picture. So Bettman, a stiff, intransigent suit interested primarily in the bottom line, isn't a poster child for all that's wonderful in sports. So he oversaw a league that, for the first time in North American pro sports history, closed its doors for an entire season, causing financial pain to thousands of vendors and ticket sellers and stadium personnel, not to mention emotional trauma for hockey fans and all of Canada. So he comes across as emotionally cold and even a little smarmy. He won. He is the cham-pion, he is the cham-pion!"

- Wayne Gretzky on the feelings of the day during the 2005 lockout: "When emotions are high, things are said, things are done. Ultimately, these players want to play. I know too many of them love the game too much."

- Bettman on the game one year after the 2004–05 lockout: "Now the team's ability to compete is based upon its hockey, front office and team-building skills, not on the team's ability to pay. We have emerged as partners with our players and our fans."

- Bettman on the signing of the television contract with Outdoor Life Network: "OLN is anticipating, as are we, subscriber growth."

- Detroit Red Wings defenseman Ian White on Bettman during the 2012 lockout: "He's an idiot."

- NHL deputy commissioner Bill Daly during the 2012 lockout: "We were extremely disappointed to have to make today's announcement. The game deserves better, the fans deserve better and the people who derive income from their connection to the NHL deserve better."

- Jesse Spector, writer of the *Sporting News*, on players hating Gary Bettman during the 2012 lockout: "Just been reading some player tweets. And you thought *you* didn't like Gary Bettman..."

- Jim Devellano, Red Wings senior vice president to Island Sports News: "The owners can basically be viewed as the ranch, and the players, and me included, are the cattle. The owners own the ranch and allow the players to eat there. That's the way it's always been and that's the way it will be forever. And the owners simply aren't going to let a union push them around. It's not going to happen."

- Krys Barch, of the Florida Panthers, on the 2012 lockout: "The lockout is a procedure to take from the players to pay for the NHL mistakes. Let's not allow the NHL to make any more mistakes."

- Paul Bissonette, Phoenix Coyotes player: "Gary Bettman takes a lot of heat for doing his job. Question to you is would you do what he does for eight million dollars a year?"

- Montreal Canadiens forward Brandon Prust on Bettman during the 2012 lockout: "Gary Bettman's autobiography is in stores now. It's titled 'How I Destroyed a Sport and a Nation.'"

- With no *Hockey Night in Canada*, Don Cherry was left to discover what else Canada has to offer: "I went to see Gordon Lightfoot on opening night at Massey Hall. I never go to shows, but I just had to see Lightfoot. He was a beauty!"

- Gary Bettman addressing the media and their questions about Donald Fehr as former head of the baseball players union:

  > *One has nothing to do with the other. Our economics are not baseball's economics. Our game is not baseball's game. Our owners are not baseball's owners, with one or two exceptions. Our union is not baseball's union. What we do has to be crafted and suited to address hockey, to address the NHL, to address our 30 teams and our 700-plus players.*

- Donald Fehr, NHLPA executive director during the 2012 lockout: "On Wednesday, NHL commissioner Gary Bettman said that the league is losing $18 to $20 million per day during the lockout. Therefore, two more weeks of cancelled games far exceeds the current economic gap."

Glossary of NHL Terms You Had to Learn Under Bettman Rule

Antitrust litigation: Refers to a legal action related to antitrust proceedings, which are designed to identify and break down monopolies and unfair business practices in the interest of encouraging competition and ensuring that everyone in the market has an equal opportunity. This would be a last-resort tactic by the players' union if talks had broken down completely during any of the three lockouts.

Audit: A review of league finances. Bettman used the audit to prove to the NHLPA that the league was in trouble during the 2004–05 lockout. However, his audit was not a typical corporate audit because it failed to take into account luxury boxes, naming rights, arena seats and club seat revenues. This was a main sticking point during that lockout negotiation.

Board of governors: The NHL board of governors is the ruling and governing body of the league. In this context, each team is a member of the league, and each member appoints a governor (usually the owner of the club) and two alternates to the board. As of 2013, the chairman of the NHL board of governors is Boston Bruins owner Jeremy Jacobs.

Chronic traumatic encephalopathy (CTE): This is a progressive degenerative brain disease that is caused by repeated trauma to the head. It has been shown to have been one of the factors in the deaths of several young NHLers as well as a few veteran players.

Collective Bargaining Agreement (CBA): This is a contract between the NHL team owners and the National Hockey League Players Association (NHLPA) that is designed to be arrived at through labor-management negotiations. It has become the most used legal term in modern hockey.

Concussion: Although there are varying degrees of severity, a concussion is generally the result of the head getting struck and the brain bouncing around inside the skull, causing temporary to long-term effects. Never discussed until recently, concussions have become a major problem in the NHL and have led to the early exit of many star players. Too many concussions can lead to CTE (see above).

Doves: During the NHL lockouts, several team owners (the "doves") expressed taking a softer approach with the players' association, but Gary Bettman quickly brought them all in line with his way of thinking. This was evident during the 2012 lockout when several owners anonymously expressed their distress at possibly cancelling another season over percentages of money.

Draft lottery: This lottery was brought into the NHL in 1993, after it was suspected the Ottawa Senators deliberately lost games to move into last place in order to select number one pick Alexandre Daigle. Prior to 1993, the top picks were based on where a team finished in the regular season. Now, when the regular season ends, the 14 NHL teams not qualifying for the playoffs are entered in a weighted lottery to determine the initial draft picks in the first round, seeded according to regular-season standing. The 30th-place team has the best chance of winning the lottery while the 29th-place team has an 18.8 percent chance of winning, with odds diminishing to 0.5 percent for the 17th-place team. The remaining order is determined by the Stanley Cup playoff results.

Drop-dead date: A provision that set the last day of contract negotiations during all three lockouts. If an agreement is not reached between the NHL and NHLPA before this date, the season is cancelled. In 2004–05, the drop-dead date passed, and the season was lost.

Escrow: This is the amount of money the players pay throughout the season based on an estimate of what hockey-related revenue (HRR) will be at the end of it. Once the final HRR is known, if the money paid out to the players by the owners was more than the players' share, the difference comes out of the escrow account. If there is anything left, the players each get a check.

Expansion: Expansion occurs when the NHL adds new teams to the league. When a new team enters the league, they must pay an expansion fee in the millions of dollars that is then distributed to the other teams already in the league and to the NHL itself. Under Gary Bettman, the league has added the Florida Panthers, Anaheim (Mighty) Ducks, Nashville Predators, Atlanta Thrashers, Columbus Blue Jackets and Minnesota Wild. Possible future expansion might include Quebec City, Seattle, Las Vegas and Saskatoon.

Fans: The people that sit in the arena seats and pay good money to watch games, buy merchandise and support their team. They are the ones often forgotten during lockouts.

FoxTrax Puck: The awful, glowing puck that was on Fox Network's broadcast of NHL games from 1996 to 1998.

Hawks: Although some team owners sought to make peace with the NHLPA during the lockouts, other owners (the "hawks") wanted to completely break the players' union. Chief among them was Boston Bruins owner Jeremy Jacobs.

Heritage Classic: A series of outdoor regular-season NHL games played between two Canadian teams. The first took place in November 2003 between the Montreal Canadiens and the Edmonton Oilers. The event is usually preceded by an exhibition game between the two clubs' old-timer legends.

Hockey-related revenue (HRR): The fixed relationship between the NHL's revenues and the amount that is available to be paid out to players. Hockey-related revenues are the money that is generated from revenue streams that are directly or indirectly related to the playing of NHL games, including ticket sales, concession sales, broadcasting agreements and so on. In addition, if a player's name and likeness is used (such as in video games), the player will participate in those revenue streams as well. The percentages of what was shared has been a major sticking point in all CBA negotiations.

Impasse: A point in a negotiation where the two sides fail to advance in the talks and are not willing to move any further.

Instigator rule: A rule established in 1992, but further strengthened in 2005, that gives extra penalties to players who start fights and can even be used to fine coaches for allowing fights in the final five minutes of a game. The rule remains controversial.

Insurance: During all the lockouts, when players decided to play in another league, they had to get insurance because they were locked into expensive contracts with the NHL, and if they got injured, it would cost their NHL teams a lot of money. For the average player, the estimated monthly cost of insurance was $10,000 to $25,000. For star players like Sidney Crosby, it was more like $400,000.

Kontinental Hockey League: The international hockey league that comprises teams from eight European countries, the majority of which are from Russia. It was one of the leagues where many NHL players went to play during the 2012 lockout. Prior to 2008, it was known as the Russian Superleague (founded in 1999).

Lockout: When a labor organization like the NHLPA fails to come to terms with management, the players are then figuratively locked out of arenas around the league.

Make whole: If the players agreed to have their share of revenues reduced, it would mean that they wouldn't receive the full amount to which their already-signed contracts entitled them. To address the issue, the NHL proposed to begin the new CBA by making a temporary cut to salaries in existing contracts. Salaries would be reduced in the first two years, to help teams adjust to the new system. But those salaries would be "made whole" via deferred payments in future years. These "make whole" or "transition" payments would be covered by teams, and would be paid over and above the players' 50 percent revenue share as calculated every season.

Mediator: An outside independent agency brought into NHL contract negotiations when both sides reach an impasse. Mediators were brought into all contract talks under Gary Bettman.

National Hockey League Players' Association (NHLPA): The unionized organization that represents hockey players in the NHL.

Quebec unions: In Canada, Quebec always does things differently. Because the province's labor laws state that a non-accredited union in the province can't be locked out, the NHLPA wanted to have the 2012 lockout deemed illegal under Quebec law, but the injunction was rejected by the Quebec Labour Board.

Research In Motion: The company that produced the BlackBerry cellphone, led by Jim Balsillie (CEO until 2012), wanted to purchase an NHL franchise and move it into the Hamilton area.

Bettman blocked every attempt by company and the owner to get a team in southern Ontario.

Restricted free agent: In principle, this means that a player is allowed to solicit offers from other teams. However, before the player signs a contract, his current club must be given a chance to match the contract and conditions. In the NHL, when one club offers a contract to a player on another team, it is often seen as an sneaky way of stealing a player, though legally so.

Revenue sharing: A type of communism for NHL franchises. Although some teams, like the Toronto Maple Leafs, are worth $1 billion, other teams such as the Edmonton Oilers and the Carolina Hurricanes do not come close. To remedy this, the league instated revenue sharing, forcing richer teams to give smaller teams a portion of their revenues.

Salary cap: An agreement or rule that places a limit on the amount of money that a sporting club can spend on player salaries. The NFL, NBA, Major League Soccer and the NHL all operate under the salary-cap system. This system allows parity between clubs and a way to control costs.

Scabs: Workers brought in to do the job of those locked out or on strike. Bettman never could replace Sidney Crosby (although if he could, he might have), but he did bring in scab referees during an NHL officials' strike.

Shootout: If the regular-season overtime period solves nothing, the game goes into a shootout. The coaches select three players from their lineup, and each player gets an open breakaway. The team with the most goals at the end of the shootout round wins the game. Reactions to the shootout have been mixed.

Small-market team: Refers to a franchise in a city that has a small population or a team that must compete for fans in a sports-saturated market such as New York City. Edmonton, Winnipeg, Carolina, New York (the Islanders) and Columbus are current examples of small-market teams.

Strike: The opposite of the lockout. A strike occurs when the labor force decides to take action and walk off the job.

Unrestricted free agent: The point in a player's career when the team that drafted him no longer retains his rights, and he can go instead to the highest bidder on the free market.

Winter Classic: The NHL's annual outdoor regular-season game. It's similar to the Heritage Classic but mostly involves American teams. The first Winter Classic in 2008 was between the Pittsburgh Penguins and the Buffalo Sabres. The game was won by the Penguins on a shootout goal by Sidney Crosby.

Notes on Sources

Web Sources

aol.sportingnews.com/nhl/story/2012-10-02/nhl-lockout-news-2012-gary-bettman-book-the-instigator-cba-negotiations

articles.latimes.com/2012/dec/15/sports/la-sp-gary-bettman-20121216

bleacherreport.com/articles/1345617-nhl-lockout-latest-winter-classic-news-proves-gary-bettman-is-wrong-man-for-nhl

blogs.edmontonjournal.com/2012/11/19/nhl-lockout-gary-bettman-enrages-influential-hockey-with-his-verbal-attack-on-journalist/

ca.sports.yahoo.com/nhl/blog/puck_daddy/post/Bettman-and-the-Jets-Tales-from-the-NHL-8217-s;_ylt=AqggrN_MilXBbcJhgEEcP8dShgM6?urn=nhl-wp6017

en.wikipedia.org/wiki/NHL_Entry_Draft

finance.yahoo.com/news/federal-mediators-join-nhl-lockout-talks-203111743--nhl.html

news.yahoo.com/bettman-says-another-nhl-lockout-looms-224124030--nhl.html

prohockeytalk.nbcsports.com/2010/06/10/maybe-gary-bettman-should-let-someone-else-hand-out-the-cup/

proicehockey.about.com/cs/history/a/nhl_suspensions.htm

slam.canoe.ca/Slam/Hockey/NHL/2011/03/10/17569601.html

sports.espn.go.com/mlb/news/story?id=4278728

sportsillustrated.cnn.com/2005/magazine/specials/sportsman/2005/11/03/gary.bettman/index.html

sportsillustrated.cnn.com/2005/writers/lester_munson/01/10/lockout.glossary/

sportsillustrated.cnn.com/hockey/nhl/news/2000/10/06/mcsorley_assault_ap/

video.foxnews.com/v/2294264382001/nhl-supports-gay-athletes-bettman-hockey-is-for-everyone/

www.businessweek.com/stories/2005-01-09/gary-bettman

www.calgaryherald.com/sports/Prime+Minister+Stephen+Harper+Gary+Bettman+stars+play+S ochi+Winter+Olympics/8217963/story.html

www.canada.com/sports/hockey/vancouver-canucks/Lockout+alphabet+from/7571077/story.html

www.canadianbusiness.com/business-strategy/
  gary-bettman-is-the-most-hated-man-in-
  hockey/

www.cbc.ca/news/canada/story/2000/10/06/
  mcsorley_verdict001006.html

www.cbc.ca/sports/hockey/nhl/story/2013/01/06/
  sp-nhl-lockout-don-cherry-coachs-corner-
  tweets.html

www.citynews.ca/2009/10/10/will-bettman-
  bring-the-nordiques-back-to-quebec/

www.ctvnews.ca/
  sports/i-m-sorry-bettman-says-to-fans-as-nhl-
  owners-vote-to-end-lockout-1.1106459

www.edmontonexaminer.com/2013/01/05/sim-
  mons-bettman-should-be-fired-after-the-lock-
  out

www.nhl.com/ice/news.
  htm?id=393419#&navid=nhl-search

www.nhl.com/ice/news.htm?id=503392

www.nhl.com/ice/news.
  htm?id=551645#&navid=nhl-search

www.nhl.com/ice/news.htm?id=555628

www.nhl.com/ice/recap.htm?id=2010030411

www.nhl.com/nhlhq/cba/rules_changes072205.
  html

www.hockeyinsideout.com/news/bettman-heri-tage-classic-not-a-concession-to-canada

www.nytimes.com/1993/02/02/sports/hockey-opening-day-for-nhl-s-first-commissioner.html

www.nytimes.com/2005/08/19/sports/hockey/19sandomir.html?_r=2&scp=4&sq=NHL+on+ABC&st=nyt&oref=slogin&

www.ottawacitizen.com/sports/fuss+over+Kaspars+Daugavins+last+week+shows+time+shootout+format/8111951/story.html

www.thehockeynews.com/articles/32083-Don-Cherry-feels-major-penalty-for-blindside-hits-to-head-should-work.html

www.usatoday.com/story/sports/nhl/2012/11/19/gary-bettman-winnipeg-free-press-inter-view/1714181/

www2.macleans.ca/2012/04/03/cbc-vs-nhl-goes-into-overtime/

J. Alexander Poulton

J. Alexander Poulton is a writer, photographer and genuine sports enthusiast. He's even willing to admit he has "called in sick" during the broadcasts of major sports events so that he can get in as much viewing as possible.

He has earned his BA in English literature and his graduate diploma in journalism, and has over 25 sports books to his credit, including books on hockey, soccer, golf, the Olympics and humor.